LITERARY SPROUTS

N ASHARUDEEN

Contents

Contents

Editor

Dr. N. Asharudeen
Assistant Professor
Department of English
E.G.S. Pillay Arts and Science College (Autonomous)
Nagapattinam - 611002

Preface

Space is needed to perform. Without space, not even the earth can perform its actions. This is a book with a number of analytical studies attempted by students and scholars. When I extended them my support as rain towards the fertile land, they just came up with their maiden attempts as sprouts. I believe that young people can make it if they have opportunities. So I have decided to offer them occasional opportunities to express thcir ideas. This book is named "Literary Sprouts" specially to recognise the writings of the untried and tried.

This book is comprised of the collections of different writers in various literatures, such as Margaret Atwood, Bhabani Bhattacharya, Aravind Adiga, Kamala Das, Toru Dutt, Philip K. Dick, Shashi Deshpande, William Somerset Maugham, George Bernard Shaw, Sharon Draper, Walt Whitman, Nathaniel Hawthorne, Girish Karnad, Paul Beatty, Charles Dickens, Jay Asher, Thomas Kyd, Mahesh Dattani, Jane Austen, Virginia Woolf and Ruskin Bond.

Acknowledgements

I never failed to thank HIM who controls everything in and around the world. ALLAH is not just a given name but named by HIMSELF. Out of ninety nine names refer to God in "Quran", ALLAH is a predominant name used and called by humans.

I am always thankful to my family in all situations which keeps me running like a stream, flowing like falls and united as an ocean with deep love. Additionally, I acknowledge the people who stand behind my attempts, my respected professors, friends and students.

My Special Thanks to,

Dr. S. Florence, Associate Professor, Department of English Annamalai University, Annamalai Nagar.

Mr. P. Muthukumar, Assistant Professor & Head, Department of English, E.G.S. Pillay Arts & Science College (A), Nagapattinam.

Mr. M. Balamurugan, Assistant Professor, Department of English, Swami Dayananda College of Arts & Science, Manjakkudi.

Mr. N. Subramaniyan, Assistant Professor, Sir Issac Newton College of Engineering and Technology, Pappakovil, Nagapattinam.

Mr. B. Sathiyamoorthy, Assistant Professor, Department of English, E.G.S. Pillay Arts & Science College (A), Nagapattinam.

Dr. H. Annshini, Assistant professor, Department of English, Infant Jesus Arts and Science College for Women, Mulagumudu.

CHAPTER ONE

SOCIAL CLASS AND PROPRIETY IN ATWOOD'S "ALIAS GRACE"

Abina Blessy. D,
II MA English,
Infant Jesus College of Arts and Science for Women,
Mulagumoodu.

Canadian literature deals with the multicultural country, written in languages such as Canadian, English, Canadian French, indigenous languages, and Canadian Gaelic. Canadian writers drew inspiration from geography and history, and their works reflect culture and region. Canadian literature is divided into English and French-language literature. Canadian literature mainly explores historical themes such as nature, ancestral life, the position of Canada compared to other countries in the world, etc. Canada's ethnic and cultural diversity has been reflected in literature since the 1980s. Canadian literature was viewed as the world's best in the 1990s.

Some of the famous Canadian writers are Alice Munro, Lucy Maud, Yann Martel, Michael Ondaatje, Mordecai Richler, Margaret

Laurence, Margaret Atwood, Malcolm Gladwell, Stephen Leacock, and Emma Donoghue.

Margaret Eleanor Atwood was born on November 18, 1939, and is a well-known Canadian poet, novelist, essayist, literary critic, teacher, inventor, and also an environmental activist. Her work explores various themes regarding identity, religion, myth, climate, and political power. Since 1969, she has produced 18 books of poetry, 9 collections of short fiction; 11 books of nonfiction; 18 novels, 2 graphic novels, and 8 children's books. Many of her writings were reproduced as films. Her poems are inspired by myth and fable.

Atwood is a founder of the Griffin Poetry Prize and the Writers Trust of Canada. She has won many literary awards, including the Booker prize and the National Book Critics Lifetime Achievement award. Some of her well-known popular works are *Surfacing* (1972), *The Handmaid's Tale (1985), Cats Eye* (1988), *Alias Grace* (1996), *The Blind Assassin (1996), Oryx and Crake* (2003), *The Testaments* (2019). She is a living author.

Alias Grace is a historical fiction novel by Canadian writer Margaret Atwood. It was first published in 1996 by McClelland & Stewart, and won the Canadian Giller Prize and was later shortlisted for the Booker Prize. Grace Marks, born in 1826, lived in or near Toronto from age 12 until 16, when the famous murders took place. When the novel begins, she has been incarcerated for 15 years at the Kingston Penitentiary in Kingston, Ontario. Among Toronto and Kingston society, Atwood portrays the highly moralistic, straitlaced language and behaviour of the Victorian era. By contrast, Mary Whitney's crude comments would have been shocking even among servants of that time.

The study of mental health, called "alienism," was a new development at the time. It was first taught in European universities and advocated that inmates be treated as patients rather than prisoners. Although the Victorian era was a time of some scientific progress, many Victorians were very much interested in the paranormal, supernatural, and occult. Hence, the use of mesmerism, hypnotism, or spiritualism was viewed as legitimate methods of inquiry.

Atwood has chosen Richmond Hill, Ontario as the location of the Kinnear farm within Upper Canada. In September 2009, 13 years after the book's publication, Richmond Hill unveiled Alias Grace Park, which was named after the novel.

Inspired by actual historical events, *Alias Grace* follows the story of convicted murderers Grace Marks. Born in Ireland, Grace immigrated to Canada at age twelve, along with her parents and siblings. Grace's mother died on the journey and was buried at sea, a deep loss that Grace is still grieving in adulthood, and Grace's father was an abusive alcoholic. Shortly after immigrating to Canada, Grace left her family to find work as a servant. While working at the house of Mrs. Alderman Parkinson, Grace befriended a fellow servant named Mary Whitney and was devastated when Mary died of complications from an abortion. After Mary's death, a depressed Grace ultimately takes work at the home of Mr. Thomas Kinnear in Richmond Hill. Grace had a tense relationship with Nancy Montgomery, the housekeeper and Mr. Kinnear's paramour, and with James McDermott, a hired hand at the household. However, she was on friendly terms with Jamie Walsh, a boy from a neighbouring family, and Jeremiah the peddler, a travelling salesman. In 1843, when Grace was sixteen, Mr. Kinnear and Nancy were murdered under brutal yet mysterious circumstances. Grace and McDermott were both arrested and tried for the murder of Thomas Kinnear. Since McDermott was convicted, that makes Grace deemed guilty as an accessory to murder; since McDermott and Grace were convicted, the Montgomery murder was never tried. McDermott was hanged, but Grace's sentence was commuted to life in prison.

By the time the novel begins, in 1859, Grace has been in prison for over a decade, having also spent some time in an insane asylum. She claims to have no memory of the day the murders took place, though she remembers the days leading up to and after the murders. Though she remains imprisoned, Grace works at the governor's house several days a week, where she helps the governor's wife with sewing. The Governor's wife is part of a group of people, led by Reverend Verringer, who are working to obtain a federal pardon on Grace's behalf. To strengthen his committee's argument for a pardon, Reverend Verringer enlists the help of Dr. Simon Jordan, an American, Harvard-educated doctor with dreams of opening his own privately-funded mental asylum. Dr. Jordan begins interviewing Grace regularly, hoping that allowing her to narrate her life story will help call up her lost memory of the murders. At the same time that he is conducting his interviews with Grace, Dr. Jordan guiltily begins an affair with his landlady, Mrs. Rachel Humphrey, whose husband, Major C. D. Humphrey, has abandoned her.

As Grace comes to the end of her story, Dr. Jordan begins to panic because he still cannot determine whether or not she is guilty. After speaking to the lawyer who represented Grace, Mr. Kenneth MacKenzie, and visiting Mr. Kinnear's home in Richmond Hill, Dr. Jordan agrees to allow Dr. Jerome DuPont, a friend of Reverend Verringer's, to hypnotise Grace. During the hypnosis, Grace begins speaking in Mary Whitney's voice. Mary Whitney admits to possessing Grace and killing Nancy, accounting for Grace's lack of memory about the murders and several sleepwalking spells that Grace had since Mary died.

Dr. Jordan realises that he is trapped. He cannot write a report detailing the hypnosis session because he will be seen as a quack and his dreams of opening his own asylum will be quashed. He also knows that Reverend Verringer will not let him off without writing a report on behalf of the Committee. Panicked about his situation, and distressed by his many interviews with Grace, Dr. Jordan persuades Rachel Humphrey that he is ill and needs her to fetch him a doctor. While she is gone, Dr. Jordan escapes back to the States on a train.

Dr. Jordan becomes tacitly engaged to a woman his mother picks out for him. At the outbreak of the Civil War, Dr. Jordan enlists as a military surgeon. He sustains a head injury and, according to his mother, loses his memory of his time in Canada. However, despite his claim to not remember treating Grace, Mrs. Jordan admits that her son mistakenly refers to his betrothed as Grace.

After twenty-eight years of imprisonment, Grace receives a pardon in 1872. She is transported to Ithaca, New York, where she marries Jamie Walsh, now a widower. At the close of the novel, Grace is on the verge of her forty-sixth birthday.

Part of Atwood's critique of the rigid class structure of the Victorian era is her exploration of how deeply ingrained notions of "proper" behaviour were then and how central they were to people's identities. While propriety is certainly influenced by gender, Atwood uses Grace's narration to suggest that proper behaviour is often even more determined by class. Atwood thus explores the way that class inexorably shapes her characters' identities, while also providing examples of how characters like Grace subtly redefine the social norms that bind them.

Grace understands her relationships with others according to their relative class status. For example, the tension between Grace and Nancy Montgomery arose from class differences, rather than from romantic rivalry, as the newspapers have convinced people. For the most part, Grace buys into the class hierarchy of her society. She disapproves of Nancy's relationship with Mr. Kinnear because she feels it violates class distinctions: Nancy is at once acting above her station, by romancing a gentleman, and below it, by taking on tasks that Grace feels shouldn't fall to her. This can be seen when Nancy insists on taking Mr. Kinnear's coffee. By showing that Grace has a deep sense of class consciousness and can articulate it—even if she is not very critical of the class system itself—Atwood shows that she is much more intelligent and savvy than the newspapers have made her out to be.

- Grace compares the upper-class women here to jellyfish, meaning that they consist of nothing much; they are insubstantial. This view of the upper-class women, as primarily ornamental, ethereal, and not very useful, fits with what Mary

> Whitney has taught Grace about the upper classes. Though upper-class, just like working-class and lower-class women, they have no power, other than their beauty, and little influence.(21-22)

Though Grace's understanding of class is, for the most part, conventional, Atwood also shows how Grace uniquely subverts the class hierarchy. Though the prison guards technically hold a higher place in society than she does as a convicted murderer, Grace describes the prison guards who consistently harass and assault her as being of low class. She also consistently makes snide comments about class. This comment gestures toward the fact that people of the upper class have a much easier time imposing their opinions on others—and that they can easily deflect both criticism and punishment because of their economic and social clout in society. Atwood thus depicts Grace as being aware of the limits and inequities of the class system, even as she largely buys into this system.

While Grace largely accepts class norms, Mary Whitney becomes the vessel for Atwood's class critique, dismantling the illusion of the upper class being superior. In contrast to her upper-class counterparts, Mary is heavily associated with bodily experience. Not only does Mary teach Grace about menstruation, but she more symbolically represents the idea of embodiment via her favourite game, in which she would hide amongst the laundry line and give out a moaning sound in order to scare Grace. Atwood depicts Mary as a self-assured person squeezing the joy out of her mundane life, but she also clearly shows how Mary's embrace of her bodily experience represents a violation of the social code. Mary suffers the ultimate punishment for her indiscretion: she dies from a botched abortion.

- Grace describes her difficulty in understanding and defining her identity. She does not know who she is because she cannot remember what she has done. These conflicting views, imposed

> on her from the outside, complicate and confuse her process of growth and self-identification. It is important to remember that Grace is barely sixteen years old when the murders occur; she certainly is not an adult. (23)

Mary also subverts class norms via her understanding of the relative power of the upper and lower classes. She explains to Grace that fancy homes have two staircases, not so the servants can be out of the way of their employers.While Atwood never explicitly endorses Mary's opinion of her power, she emphasises how much Grace knows about how to get along in the world—from her sewing expertise to everyday practical knowledge, such as the impossibility of making butter when there is a thunderstorm. Atwood contrasts Grace's vast and varied practical knowledge with Dr. Jordan's helplessness in caring for himself, such as when he goes to market instead of his sick landlady and is clueless about how to procure food. In addition to being inherently gendered, they emphasise the upper class' extreme dependence on their servants; Atwood thus imbues servants like Grace with a substantial amount of power, even if it is not quite as much as Mary Whitney imagines for herself.

Atwood makes a nuanced argument about class, emphasising how notions of propriety—acting according to one's class status—are deeply comforting to Grace, even as they ostensibly limit her. At the same time, Atwood also gives voice to the way that characters like Grace, and more obviously Mary Whitney, quietly critique or invert the social codes of class behavior, even as they continue to live their lives according to these codes.

Reference

Atwood, Margaret. *Alias Grace.* "Author's Afterword": McClelland & Stewart. 1996.

Atwood, Margaret. "In Search of Alias Grace: On Writing Canadian Historical Fiction". *American Historical Review.* 1998.103 (5): 1515.

CBC, Netflix to screen miniseries based on Margaret Atwood novel *Alias Grace.* The Globe and Mail, June 21, 2016.

Dominic, K. V. Studies in Contemporary Canadian Literature. Pinnacle Technology. 2010. pp. 8–9.

Katz, Briget "The Mysterious Murder Case That Inspired Margaret Atwood's 'Alias Grace". *Smithsonian Magazine*. November 2017.

Keith, W. J. Canadian Literature in English. The Porcupine's Quill. 2006.

New, William H. Encyclopedia of Literature in Canada. University of Toronto Press. 2002. pp. 259–261.

R.G. Moyles, ed. Improved by Cultivation: English-Canadian Prose to 1914. Broadview Press. 1994.

"Sarah Polley to adapt Margaret Atwood's Alias Grace" Archived 5 January 2012 at the Library of Congress Web Archives. National Post, January 4, 2012.

CHAPTER TWO

INTERSECTIONS OF GENDER AND SOCIETY IN ATWOOD'S FEMINIST DYSTOPIAN NOVEL: "THE HANDMAID'S TALE"

Ajitha Robin. I,
II MA English,
Infant Jesus College of Arts and Science for Women,
Mulagumoodu.

This research has made an attempt to make analytical study on Feminist dystopia exists in the novel *The Handmaid's Tale* by Margaret Atwood. It was published in the year 1985. It talks about gender inequality and domestic politics. In a dystopian society, women are controlled by free thought and action. The dystopian genre examines a negative outlook on life, intimidation, the loss of free will and individuality, and harassment. Dystopia is a word that is used to describe a terrible world where women live in difficulty and their existence frequently ends in death. Atwood's novel explains the circumstances that are taking place in a dystopian future, where an oppressive government invades power and compels women to fight for their rights.

The Handmaid's Tale is regarded as a feminist work that is liberal. This book contains a critique of feminism. Atwood attended an interview at Random House, she stated about the book, "This is a book about the logical conclusion of women that occurs certain casual attitudes that held" (Interview). Atwood's writings always point out the female characters struggling with the harsh social structures; she pushed herself to attend another interview, in which she defines her opinion of feminism in universal terms, "as the equality of humans and liberty of choice." Despite the fact that on the surface, *The Handmaid's Tale* seems to be sexist and anti-feminist, Atwood gives her point of feminist opinion through deep analysis. It is evident to show the support of women's empowerment and gender equality because it depicts a dystopian society where the restriction of gender-bias points out the dreadfulness.

The Handmaid's Tale is an example of speculative fiction because it infers an alternate society that is removed and distant from its culture. In the novel, Atwood satirises the various aspects she pointed out in the 1980s: poor treatment of women, illness, infertility, and the deterioration of religion. by imagining a near-future, rather than a distant erasure from our society. The novel analyses the valid outcomes of surviving things. For example, the novel illustrates what would go on if modern society's increasingly permissive behaviour toward sex and sexuality incited a serious backlash, favouring political groups who recognise the repression and control of women's sexuality. The *Handmaid's Tale* indicates that the growth of spiritual liberty, together with a decreasing delivery ratio, could stimulate a totalitarian administration in the United States.

Atwood's novel occurs as part of a robust tradition of feminist dystopian fiction that scrutinises the intersections of gender and society in provoking and imaginative ways. It analyses the warning opinions that reflect the gender inequality present in contemporary society by showing the existence of body shaming, the light value of women in society, the weakness of private temperament, and the repression of women by other women.

Atwood asserts that her novel was not calculated as a feminist work. She wants to give women's voices through the dystopian genre. The novel points out that a woman called Offred is compelled to live as a handmaid. In totalitarian North America, she is forced to deliver a child against her will. It is represented by a former community named Gilead, in which women, particularly productive women, are prevented. Most of the basic rights of women have been taken away from their belongings and followed by the new form of government authority. This occurs on a large scale when the commander lets Offred enjoy some relaxation, but also on a larger scale when, towards the end of the novel, Offred plans to secretly flee from the community.

The Handmaid's Tale insists that lawfully regulating women's reproductive liberation is wrong both morally and politically. The Gileadean government's intention was to own and control women's fertility in society, which affected Offred and the other Handmaids.The women in Gilead society can be split into six groups: handmaids, wives, Marthas, Aunts, Econowives, and Unwomen. Their dress code is based on their category, Handmaids wear the red colour, dull green is for the Marthas, Econowives wear cheap and skimpy lined dresses, and Widows wear black.

In the Gileadean society, women didn't identify their original name; they were commonly known as "Of"and the connected name belonged to the commander. Offered means *Of-Fred* because she is entirely the property of the commander Fred and her rights have been erased.

Atwood's dystopia shows that women act as the toys of men. Offered is dressed like a harlot and visits a prostitute's resort,

Jezebel's. In that place, women are dressed up as sex dolls for men to be entirely used for their sexual happiness. It shows women as sex items, sex toys, and maternal or domestic employees.

Moira, who was a lesbian feminist extremist, is eventually reduced to the role of a prostitute in the role of Jezebel. The manifestation of Atwood's dystopia is very dark because women do not see the ability to carry out revolutions to free themselves from the prisons imposed by patriarchy in society. As Moira's fate shows in Jezebel, she is described as defeated and relinquished to her destiny. She is almost a toy in the hands of men. Atwood's dystopia is ultimately pessimistic, it does not provide a radical alternative to patriarchy; and while men are imprisoned and oppressed, only men have the power in society to allow women to move freely beyond their roles engraved by patriarchal society. As consensual or rebellious against domination, women must be at the mercy of men for their imprisonment or release and be dependent on them. "This is a reconstruction. All of it is a reconstruction. It's construction now, in my head, as I lie flat on my single bed rehearsing what I should or shouldn't have done, how I should gave plated it if I ever get out of here" (144).

The above quote hints that, Offred is forced into a state of negotiation with the male power and has to play within its boundaries, at the mercy of the male power. Atwood strictly adheres to the terms of Offred and considers the possibility of escape from this female dystopia. Then, Nick is the one who finally rescues Offred from the dictator's tyranny. "Let's stop there. I intend to get out of here. It can't last forever. Others have thought such things, in bad times before this, and they were always right, they did get out one way or another, and it didn't last forever. Although for them it may have lasted all the forever they had" (144).

The patriarchal society committed cruelty toward Offred. She holds the power of the written word and announcements. She is a woman with the ability to forgive the sins that men have bestowed upon her. She was abused and treated as a domestic slave and a sex toy. The only opposition she has is the power to deny or confer forgiveness, which Atwood interprets as the tremendous power of all because in record, women have been silenced and this is his story. This is Offred's attempt to restore the narrative and create her story by regulating and governing the power to deny or confer forgiveness of men in many cases of abusing her.

The story of *The Handmaid's Tale* is about the utmost power that men wield over women in society. The story is an endeavour to boycott the absolute totalitarianism of male rights over female submission and intimidation.

Reference

Allana, A Callaway.*Women disunited: Margaret Atwood's The Handmaid's Tale as a Critique of feminism*, San Jose State University, SJSU. 2008.

Atwood, Margaret. *The Handmaid's Tale.* Torento, Ontario: McCleland Steward Ltd, 1985.

Callaway, Alana A. "Women disunited: Margaret Atwood's *The Handmaid's Tale* as a Critique of Feminism". San Jose: San Jose State University Press. 2008.

Chung Chin-Yi, *The Handmaid's Tale: A Feminist Dystopia*, National University of Singapore.An International Journal of English Language, Literature and Literary TheoryVol. IV Issue III, July 2015. <http://interactionsforum.com/new-academia>

Karen Stein. Margaret Atwood's Modest Proposal: The Handmaid's Tale. Margaret Atwood. Ed. Harold Bloom. Philadelphia: Chelsea House Publishers, 2000, 2001.

M. L. Eileen Brisha. "Ecofeminism and Politics of Triple Marginalization in Atwood's *The Handmaid's Tale.*" *Journal of Humanities and Social Science*, 2004.

CHAPTER THREE

AN ANALYSIS ON BHABANI BHATTACHARYA'S "MUSIC FOR MOHINI"

S. Ambika,
MA English (2020-2022),
Edayathangudy G. S. Pillay Arts & Science College (Autonomous),
Nagapattinam.

Bhabani Bhattacharya is a realist who enjoys delving into life's realities. He has a keen awareness of contemporary Indian society's concerns. Village and city are the major themes in *Music for Mohini*, which is a harmonic blending of tradition and modernity. In Mohini, Bhattacharya portrays an ideal woman whose life is divided into two phases. It is necessary in two phases to depict Mohini's adaptation and understanding in a shifting circumstance.

In a typical scene, a brother and sister fight for fun while their father is away, but when he returns, the boy claims to be working on a math problem while Mohini pretends to be reading an Ancient

India textbook. When the professor casually looks at the volume she has open in front of her and realises it is a Bangla novel, he is taken away. Lydia Languish, the protagonist of Sheridan's classic The Rivals, comes to mind. The Old Mother realises that Mohini is no longer a child, but a woman, and she advises her son to marry her as soon as possible.

As a result of the bridegroom's suggestion, one proposal arrives through the agency of a bangle-seller, who is a gorgeous, well-educated affluent young man in his late twenties named Jayadev, who is the head of the family known as the Big House in the village Behula. Old Mother and Mohini agree that the pairing is ideal. Only her father hesitates. How can his city-bred, freedom-loving daughter be happy in a village among the old-world folk? The match has been accepted by Jayadev's mother since she has determined that the Mohini's palm has all eight indications of luck, such as the wheel's fingers, the conch, the elephant, and so on.

The marriage has been agreed upon, and the traditional observances will take place prior to the wedding. After exchanging final vows behind the protective bridal covering, husband and wife saw each other for the first time: Jayadev stared, as Mohini's head sank, her face flushed. His appearance didn't signify anything. She merely wished for his acceptance and happiness.

Mohini departs from this family, which is filled with love, security, wit, wisdom, laughter, music, and traditional customs have surrounded her throughout her life. She may think of Old Mother's parting remarks many times in the years to come. Respect your mother-in-law as if she were your own mother, and follow her wishes. Respond to her fiery comments with complete silence. "Sweeten your speech when you talk to your neighbours. Words dipped in honey cost nothing. Bend yourself to the customs and traditions of the village...." (*Music for Mohini*, 90).

The scholar Jayadev sees Mohini as a link between India's history and future. Will she not grow into a modern-day Maitreyi, the epitome of Vedic womanhood, smart and powerful, and an equal partner in the effort to make life meaningful and free? Mohini is torn between being too modern for some prospects and being too traditional for others. Mohini leaves her sophisticated Calcutta home for the historic Big House in Behula village.

Mohini's mother-in-law encourages her to avoid wearing face powder, sleeveless blouses, and glass bangles. She demands that she only perform religious songs and wear a simple cotton saree. Even the way she wears her hair is dictated by tradition. The presence of the forefathers seems to pervade the dwelling. The widowed mother-in-law keeps a collection of her late husband's wooden sandals in the family prayer room and worships them on a daily basis.

Mohini, a city-bred and village-wed enlightened girl, must play a key part in transforming Big House and the village. Rooplekha, her sister-in-law, who is village-bred and city-married, highlights the role that their situation requires them to play in the restoration of a free India.

Women in the House are subject to specific restrictions. The mistress of the House is not permitted to leave the house. Even when Jayadev is bitten by a snake, Mohini's mother refuses to let her walk in public. The bride enters the village solely in a palanquin, according to Big House tradition. In a palanquin, Mohini also enters the village. The women of the House are not permitted to eat at the same table as the males. Music is only tolerated in the context of worship. It is part of the House's tradition to preserve the family.

Rooplekha shares her own experience with Mohini. For Rooplekha, the city is as cruel to a foreigner as the country is to Mohini. There isn't any more, and there isn't any less. And Rooplekha makes a concerted effort to adapt to city life. She had to marry a lad of equal standing because she was a maid of the Big House. Because no one acceptable in Bengal countryside could be found, the mother handed her against her will to a city youth, a surgeon at a Calcutta Medical College. She was only sixteen years old at the time. Smart women with enamelled faces came to visit her, and they gave her a glance and sobbed humorously over her beauty and the old fashioned sari and blouse. They were also amused by her country accent. In a nutshell, she was a barbarian and a misfit for them. She was a vegetarian before moving to the city, where she was expected to consume eggs, fish, and meat. It was difficult for her to move around with her face exposed and openly mingle with his pals.

She tells Mohini that she'll have to adapt herself in the opposite direction. She needs to clear her mind of its comfortable city furnishings, so to speak, or else there will be a lot of nasty language and disdainful behaviour. Mohini is perplexed by the objective of Rooplekha and expresses her city's opinion that such fussing should be avoided because, in her opinion, Mohini receives the basic word of their marriage from Rooplekha, the village-bred, wiser, and experienced girl:

- Shall I answer you? We who're so wed serve some real purpose. It's as though we made a bridge between two banks of a river. We connect culture with culture, Mohini, our old Eastern view of life with the new semi-Western outlook. The city absorbs a little of the 'barbaric' village, the village absorbs a little of the 'West-polluted' city. Both change, unaware. They are less angry with each other. This is more urgent today than even before. (*Music For Mohini*, 126-27)

In the story of Harindra's family, there is yet another battle between old and modern principles. Harindra's father, the elderly Kaviraj, is an Ayurvedic physician, whereas his son, Harindra, is a surgeon who received his education and training in a western-style medical school. The old father frequently debates with his son on the millennium-long dominance of Ayurveda. The old guy offers Ayurvedic medicine to his wife and never lets his son cure her. Harindra argues "There are many good drugs in our Ayurvedic system. We know them, we use them, not the home products but those made in modern laboratories. What's wrong in using in the fight against disease the best that east and west have to offer? Medicine knows no race or nationality." (*Music For Mohini*, 166).

Bhattacharya reconciles old values and systems with modern values and systems through the story of Harindra.

After a few days, Harindra informs mother of Mohini's pregnancy. She recognises that this is the generation of young men and women, with their new values and ambitions. To cope with the new age, she begins to alter her beliefs. Finally, the mother agrees that her son's route is the right one, and she sees her son clearly for the first time. His views, his new point of view, shaped by the new spirit in the region, were different and opposing to hers, but they were still true values. With the passage of time, Mohini realises that the Mother does not lack basic virtues such as compassion and sacrifice. Jayadev and her mother-in-law make her proud. As stated at the outset, the novel, *Music For Mohini*, depicts a woman's sacrifice of her comforts for the purpose of the nation's societal and cultural progress on the basis of ideals by the sacrifice of woman by adjusting herself in eccentricities properly. The study depicts how a lady accepts other practises and traditions in order to create a prospective society free of old fetters and confidence in fraternity.

Reference

Bhattacharya, Bhabani. *Music For Mohini*. New Delhi: Published in Orient Paperbacks, 1952.

CHAPTER FOUR

Why is "Fall of Mankind"? - A Theological Review

Amos Dishonraj. A,
II MA English,
Edayathangudy G. S. Pillay Arts & Science College (Autonomous),
Nagapattinam.

Introduction

In the beginning, the earth was without form and the darkness was over the face of the deep. And the spirit of God was hovering over the surface of the water. Then God decided to correct the earth. He took six days to create all the oceans, seas, land, trees, species and every livestock.

The Six Days of Creation

On the first day of creation, God wanted to remove darkness from the world, and so he said, "Let there be light" (Genesis 1:3), and there was light. God saw light was good. God separated the light from the darkness; he called the light as 'day' and darkness as 'night'.

On the second day of creation, God created expanse of heaven and extended the space between heaven and the water.

On the third day of creation, God planned to separate water and land. Water covered all over the world, there was no land .The earth was filled with water. And so God said, "let the water under the heavens be gathered together into one place and let the dry land appear" (Genesis 1:9). And God called the dry land as Earth, and gathering together of the waters as 'seas'

On the same day, God planned to create the vegetation. And so he said, "Let the earth sprout vegetation, plants yielding seed and fruit trees bearing fruit in which are their seeds, each according to its kind on the earth" (Genesis 1:11).

On the fourth day of creation, God said, "Let there be lights in the expanse of the heaven to separate day and night, and then be for signs and seasons and for days and years. And let them be lights in the expanse of the heavens to give lights upon the earth" (Genesis 1:14-15). And God made two great lights. The greater light to rule the day called 'Sun' and the lesser light to rule night and called 'moon'. And God set them in the expanse of heavens to give light on the earth, to rule over the day and night, and to separate the light from the darkness.

On the fifth day of creation, God planned to create aquatic creatures, birds and animal species. God said, "Let the water swarm with living creatures and let birds fly above the earth" (Genesis 1:20). And God blessed them saying, "Be fruitful and multiply and fill the waters and the earth" (Genesis 1:22).

The Creation of Man

On the sixth day of creation, God said, "Let us make man in our image, after our likeness, and let them have dominion over the fish of the sea, over birds of the heaven, over the livestock and over all the earth and over every creepy thing that creeps on the earth. So, God created man in his own image" (Genesis 1:26-27). God created man with dust of the ground and breathed into his nostrils the breath of life and man became a living being. God named him as Adam, father of all humans.

After these, God rested on the seventh day.

The Garden of Eden

God planted a garden in the East called Eden. And there he put the man whom he had formed. And God made to spring up every tree that is pleasant to sight and also good for food. There he made to spring up "The tree of life" in the midst of the garden and "The tree of knowledge of good and evil" (Genesis 2:9).

There are four rivers flowing out of Eden to water the garden namely 'PISHON' 'GIHON' 'TIGRIS' and 'EUPHRATES'.

God's Command

The Lord God took the man and put him in the garden of Eden, to work it and keep it. And God commanded the man saying, "You may surely eat of every tree of the garden, but of the tree of the knowledge of good and evil you shall not eat, for on the day that you eat, you shall surely die" (Genesis 2:16-17).

Creation of Eve

Then the God said, "It is not good that the man should be alone, I will make him a helper for him. So God caused a deep sleep for the man, and he took one of Adam's ribs and closed up its place with flesh.

And the rib that the Lord God had taken from the man, he made into a woman and brought her to the man. The man said,

This at last is bone of my bones
And flesh of my flesh;
She shall be called woman
Because she was taken out of men. (Genesis 2:23)

The Fall of Men

'The Satan's temptation' Satan, who wanted to ruin the creature of God, entered the garden as disguised as a serpent. He started tempting Eve. He said to the woman, "Did God actually say 'you shall not eat of any tree in the garden?" (Genesis 3:1). And the woman said to the serpent, "We may eat of the fruit of the trees in the garden, but God said 'you shall not eat of the fruit of the tree that is in the midst of the garden', neither shall you touch it, lest you die" (Genesis 3:2-3). But the serpent tempted the woman, "you will not surely die" (Genesis 3:4). God knows that when you eat of it, your eyes will be opened and you will be like God and goddess, and knowing good and evil. (Genesis 3:5).

Eve Ate the Fruit

Eve saw that the tree was good for food, and it was delight to the eyes, and that the tree was to be desired to make one wise; she started to describe the fruit,

Here grows the cure of all, this fruit divine,
Fair to the eye, inviting to the taste,
Of virtue to make wise: What hinders then
To reach, and feed at once both body and mind?
So saying, her rash hand in evil hour
Forth reaching to the fruit,she plucked,she eat!
Earth felt the wound; and Nature from her seat,
Sighing through all her works, gave signs of woe. (Paradise Lost, Book IX , Line 776-783) .

She took of its fruit and ate, and she also gave some to her husband, He ate. They both got rid of innocence, earth suffered ,

Earth trembled from her entrails, as again
In pangs; and Nature gave a second groan;
Sky loured; and, muttering thunder, some sad drops
Wept at completing of the mortal sin. (Paradise Lost, Book IX, Line
1000-1004)

Then the eyes of both were opened and they came to know, they were naked, and they sewed fig leaves together and made themselves to cover their body.

Judgment of the God

In the Evening of the day, they heard the sound of the God who was walking in the garden. And the man and his wife hide themselves from the presence of God among the trees of the garden. But god called out the man, "where are you?" (Genesis 3:9) And he said, "I heard the sound of you in the garden, and I was afraid because I was naked" (Genesis 3:10). God asked, "Who told you that you were naked? Have you eaten the tree of which I commanded you not to eat? " (Genesis 3:11). The man said, "the woman gave me fruit of the tree, and I ate" (Genesis 3:12), God asked the woman, "what is this that you have done?" (Genesis 3:13), the woman said, "The serpent deceived me and I ate".

The Lord God said to the serpent,
Because you have done this,
Cursed are you above all livestock
And above all beasts of the field;
On your belly you shall go,
And dust you shall eat
All the days of your life" (Genesis 3:14)

The Lord God said to the woman, "I will surely multiply your pain in child bearing; in pain you shall bring forth children, your desire shall be for your husband, and he shall rule over you" (Genesis 3:16).

And to Adam,

Because you have listened to the voice of your wife, and have eaten of the tree, cursed is the ground because of you, in pain you shall eat of it all the days of your life; thorns and thistles it shall bring forth for you and you shall eat the plants of the field, by the sweat of your face, you shall eat bread, till you return to the ground, for out of it you were taken;for you are dust, and to dust you shall return. (Genesis 3:17-19)

Then the god said, "Behold, the man has become like one of us in knowing good and evil, Now, lest he reach out his hand and take also 'the tree of life' and eat and live forever". Therefore, God sent him out from the garden of Eden, from which he was taken. And God secured the garden with 'cherubin' and a 'flaming sword' that turned every way to guard the way to "the tree of life " (Genesis 3:22-24).

What is the plan of God?

These are history of evolution of mankind with reference to *The Bible.*

And we came to know,
"What is the plan of God?"

"Why did he create the earth?"

"Why did he create humans?"

"Why did he spring up 'the forbidden tree' along with 'the tree of life'?"

If God does not plant 'the forbidden tree', no one gets tempted; If no one gets tempted, no one can commit sins; If no one could commit sins, there is no need for Jesus Christ's crucifixion for the sin of the people.

The Lord God is the creator of the entire universe. He knows what is going to happen next. He already knew everything; he knew that man would fall. And God also needs that fall of mankind. Without the fall, they couldn't get rid of their innocence; there would be no more generation behind Adam and Eve. You don't know me and I you.

Conclusion

So, the fall of man was necessary there, and so, the mankind rose with sins, mankind grew with seven deadly sins such as: pride, greed, lust, envy, gluttony, wrath and sloth to rectify the sins "Jesus Christ" were crucified. The Lord God gave his only son to remove the sins of the people, which were planted in the Garden of Eden.

Reference

The Bible, The Old Testament.

CHAPTER FIVE

Caste Discrimination in Aravind Adiga's "The White Tiger"

I. Ashika,
II MA English,
Infant Jesus College of Arts and Science for Women,
Mulagumoodu.

This paper depicts caste discrimination in the novel *The White Tiger* by Aravind Adiga. Caste discrimination in modern times has been converted into a class system. The novel also shows the dangerous consequences of this discrimination on society. The caste system is still vibrantly practised in many villages and also in the cities of India. In India a developing country, there are diverse religious people living together, but still a caste system exists. India holds a very rich tradition in culture and marriage. But people who really live here can tell how this culture, religion, rules, and caste are affecting people and stealing their lives. Poor and rich people are also separated in India by this caste system.

Aravind Adiga's Booker Prize winning novel *The White Tiger* (2008) explores the controversial issues of caste discrimination vividly in the setting of the 1990s economically booming modern India. Adiga has shown how caste discrimination has usurped the whole society, where the low-caste people are deprived of the basic rights of free citizens, like education and health. Mulk Raj Anand, Salman Rushdie, Kiran Nagarkar and Adiga try to depict the problems of Indian underdogs.

In his novel, Aravind Adiga presents the Indian caste system. He describes how lower caste people are insulted and forced to work for others in society, as well as how the caste system persists in rural India.A person who is born in one particular caste and that caste to which he belongs will determine his occupation. Balram Halwai was born into a poor family from the Halwai caste. The caste indicates the sweet maker community. He was called Munna, which has the meaning of boy, and later a school teacher called him "White Tiger". He was born in the small village of Laxmangarh. Aravind Adiga said that Laxmangarh was a region in dark India where the rich landlords owned all the benefits of agriculture and they used to exploit the poor, innocent, downtrodden people mercilessly. Balram's family is a poverty stricken family, and his neighbours were under the domination of the rich landlords. Balram faces many problems due to caste discrimination in education, employment, religion, freedom, and poverty. All these are portrayed through the life of Balram Halwai .Poor people like Balram can't break through the barriers of poverty, caste discrimination, and culture because the rich get richer and the poor get poorer.

Like Balram and other thousands of people unable to finish school due to caste discrimination and poverty, Balram never finishes his schooling. The low caste people like Balram face many problems while pursuing their education, Balram's grandmother Kusum also wants to stop his education, so she told her son Vikram Halwai to stop his son's education and "put him to work in the tea shop and let him make some money" (28).

Balram goes to work with his brother in the teashop. Due to poverty, he breaks coal and wipes tables in the tea shop. He knows very well that if he stays in the tea shop, he will not get any opportunity to make his life better. So Balram asks his grandmother to pay for him, so he can take driving lessons. Kussum his grandmother, agrees to send him to take driving lessons, and Balram promises that he will send his monthly salary if he gets a job. Balram visits all the taxi stands and begs the drivers to teach him for free, but they don't accept him. Finally, Balram and his brother met an old man, and he accepted to teach him. The old man asked Balram about his caste: it can be evident in these lines,

- "What caste are you?"
- 'Halwai'
- 'Sweet-maker, the old driver said, shaking his head that a what you people do? You make sweets. How can you learn to drive? He pointed his bookah at the live coals that's like getting coals to make ice for you. Mastering a car he moved the stick of an invisible gearbox-it's like turning a wild stallion only a boy from the warrior castes can manage that. You need to have. Aggression in your blood. Muslim, Rajputs, Sikhs- they're fighters, they can became drivers. You think sweet-makers can last long in fourth gear? (56)

Whenever Balram made mistakes, the old driver slapped Balram on his head and treated Halwai badly due to his warrior caste. The old driver says Halwai is not a warrior caste and reveals that Balram belongs to the sweet maker caste, and he says to Balram, "why don't you stick to sweet and tea?" (56). Wherever he goes, his destiny follows him. As he finishes his training, the old driver can't help him to find a job. Balram knows that he will find it difficult to get a job except in tea shops because society judges that he can only make sweets and a man is known and recognised only by his caste. The life of a poor person becomes worse due to the judgement of society. After finishing his training, Balram knocks on the door of the rich mansion to search for a job. Finally, Balram gets a job in a stork mansion. He is appointed as a driver for Stork's son Ashok.

Stork again asked the similar question which the old driver asked to Balram "What caste is that top or bottom" (62). Even high caste men are allowed to work in the Stork mansion. Balram also knows his caste is bestowed through this question. As it is revealed in the novel,

See, Halmai, My name means "sweet maker". That's my caste-my destiny. Everyone in the darkness who hears that name knows all about me at once. That's why Kishan and I kept getting a job at sweet shops where ever we went. The owner thought, Ah, they're making sweets and tea is in their blood. (63)

Balram exposes the pitiable condition of a servant living in Delhi, and he knows that he is destined to be a sweet maker. That's why Balram and his brother Kisan only get jobs at tea shops. Balram's father is a rickshaw puller, but he is not a sweet maker. Balram's father was supposed to inherit the shop, but due to the people from another caste, they never allowed him. They have stolen it with the help of some police, and this is the reason why his father did not become a sweet maker. In addition, Balram also reveals the rich and the poor: "in the olden days here were one thousand castes and destines in India. These days, there are just two castes: men with Big bellies and men with small bellies" (64). The caste system also divides everyone into high and low social status. But for Balram there are two castes: those with big bellies and those with small bellies. Only the rickshaw pullers, servants, coolies, drivers, and workers have small bellies. It shows that India still has a caste system and poverty is still present in India. So he breaks down his own views as, "It didn't matter whether you were a woman or a Muslim, or an untouchable, anyone with a big belly could rise up" (64) Mr. Mukesha, son of Stork, treats Balram as inferior to dogs. Because of his low birth, Balram is treated as an animal, and his job is to carry all the shopping bags of his master, and he has to do all the menial jobs. This situation is stated by Balram in the following lines:

- The rich expect their dogs to be treated like human, you see they expect their degan be Pampered and walked, and petted and even washed and guess who had do the Washing? I got down on my knees and began scrubbing the dogs and then lathering them and then washing them down and taking a blow dryer and drying their skin. (78)

Balram accepted him as a driver as well as that he belongs to the Halwai caste. He says, "I was a servant once you see only three nation have never let themselves be ruled by foreigner's China Afghanistan and Abyssinia" (5). After getting freedom from the Britishers, in India, these low-caste men are still ruled by their masters, and their bodies tell the history of their life and sufferings due to poverty. If a low caste man becomes a socialist in society, the upper caste men like storks bow down the head before them. Balram describes with wonder how his childhood hero, Vijay, a pig farmer's son, turned out to be a wealthy politician. Balram says, "I waited by the gate and watched. The stork himself came out to see Vijay, and bowed down before him a land lord bowing before a Pig herd's son! The marvels democracy!" (103). In public gatherings, drivers and rickshaw pullers are not allowed. The voice of the underclass is strongly said by Balram. He also realises that the discrimination between the rich and poor is felt not only in the villages but also in cities. In the village, Balram describes the lives of rickshaw pullers who become weak and unhealthy by pulling the rickshaw. And the rickshaw puller had to pay one third of the amount to the landlords. Balram's father, Vikram, was also hit by poverty, hence Balram describes his father as,

- My father's spine was a knotted rope, the kind that women use in village to pull water from wells, the clavicle curved around his neck in high relief, like a dog's collar: cuts a nicks and scar like little whip marks in his flesh, ran down his chest and waist, reaching down below his hip bones into his buttocks. The story of a poor man's life is written on his body, in a sharp pen.

(26-27)

The physiques of the rich, the poor, and the average worker differ greatly, and a person's body structure can be determined by his background. Balram's father grew up in extreme poverty, so he has a weak body and his mother dreamt of a luxurious life. In India, rickshaw pullers are restricted to certain streets and public places that enable foreigners to see them, "Rickshaw pullers are not allowed inside the part of Delhi where foreigner's might see them and gape" (5). Even though they were not allowed to sit on the chair, Balram's father preferred to stand, and it gave him respect towards his father. If the rickshaw pullers show themselves in front of the foreigners, they are seen as a burden by the foreigners. When Balram worked as a driver for Stork House, he often drove his employer to the mall. People from the low caste and their drivers are not allowed to go into such public places, and the drivers have to wait for their masters outside the mall. While they were waiting for their master, the security guards at the shopping mall easily identified them by their sandals.

The high caste people are allowed to go inside the mall and the low caste people are not allowed inside the mall because the poor man has history in his body. Balram is never taught by his parents and teachers to be clean. For the first time, Balram buys toothpaste and says, "Why had he raised me to live like an animal? Why do all the poor live amid filth, such ugliness?" (51). When Balram tries to go inside the mall, he knows that only a man who wears a T-shirt with an English word and jeans is allowed inside the mall. So he buys a T-shirt and shoes like what Mr. Ashok has, and he also hides it from Pinky and Ashok.

For caste discrimination in religion is also revealed by, Mr. Ashok's love for Pinky, who is a Christian and Mr. Ashok, is a Hindu. A Hindu man cannot marry a woman from another caste and religion, but Mr. Ashok does not care about that. They were separated because of religion and cultural differences. In India, religious discrimination is still present vibrantly. Once Stork's grandson comes out with a plastic bat and ball, his grandson calls himself Azharuddin, the former Indian Cricket Team captain. But the stork said to his grandson, call yourself Gavaskar because Azharuddin is a Muslim. Muslims and Christian are considered as untouchables in Hindu society, and they considered them to be inferior. In India, every family in mansions and apartments has servant quarters, Balram lives in a tiny room with cockroaches, are and the low caste people live in slums and also in basements. Due to poverty, they are isolated from society. This separation is described by Mulk Raj Anand in Untouchable.

- The One castes colony was a group of mud-walled houses that clustered together in two rows, under the shadow. Both of the town and cantonment, but outside their boundaries and separate from them. There lived the scavenger, the leather workers, the washer man, the barbers, the water-carrier, the grass cutters and other out castes from Hindu society. (11)

When Ashok asks Balram to drink, he responds, "no sir in my caste, we never drink."(65) People from the high caste can buy liquor, and it also shows the dominating system in India. The high-caste people don't even know how to interact with their servants. In every drink store, there are two kinds of drinks, one for the village or untouchable boys like Balram and another for rich land lords like Mr. Ashok. There is also a restriction in the food when Ashok visits his native place, and a man told him to eat chicken but Mr. Ashok liked vegetarian so a man from his place says, "you're a landlord. It's the Brahmin who are vegetarian, not us" (83). Balram also talks about the dream of the poor that they must have enough food like the rich. But the rich dream to lose of their weight like the poor. But the poor don't have to do exercise to lose their weight.

Balram then tells Mr. Jiabao about the Rooster Coop in India. When people from the lower caste are caught in a Rooster Coop they cannot easily get out of the trap. People from the low caste do not have the freedom to get out of the coop to make a better life. In India, poor people are crushed and isolated by a wealthy and powerful society. Balram tried to overcome his poor social status and also caste discrimination, so he killed his master Ashok, stole his money, and became a successful business man in Bangalore, because Bangalore is one of the major cities in India where science and technology are so advanced. He also plans to get out of the rooster coop because he was born in darkness and later came to light. While visiting a national zoo, Balram tells Dharman, "let animal live like animal, let human live like humans. That's my whole philosophy in a sentence" (276). Balram feels proud that he has done a great job by breaking the cage of the rooster coop and owes its social obstacles. He became a business man and runs a car service for a call centre in Bangalore, and also tells his driver to imitate him if they wish to succeed in their life. He also wants to build a school for poor children in Banglore and his desire for freedom also came alive after starting his own business.

India is a great country, maintaining unity in diversity, which is really a proud thing. But still, people do not accept or respect other cultures, castes, or religions. Adiga has depicted many issues in his work. One can notice that India is being confronted by most of the issues put forth by him. The caste system has become a curse on Indian society, dividing the community and creating differences between people. But some changes have happened in the minds of human beings and they have given no importance to the caste system.

Reference

Adiga, Aravind. *The White Tiger*. New Delhi: Horper Collins Publishers. 2008. Print.

Chandra, Ansul. *Reflection of India in AravindAdiga's The White Tiger*. Indian

Anand Mulk Raj. *Untouchable*. GulabVazirani for Amold Publisher, 1970.

Booker prize winners on India. Ed.Supriya Shukla. New Delhi: Atlantic, 2013.Print.

Sebastian A.J. Poor – *Rich Divide in AravindAdiga's The White Tiger*. Journal of Alternative Perspectives in the Social Sciences. Georgia. 2009.

CHAPTER SIX

PAST MEMORIES: TREASURE IN HEART

M.S. Atchaya,
II MA English,
Edayathangudy G. S. Pillay Arts & Science College
(Autonomous),
Nagapattinam,

This paper deals with the past memories of life. It can cause emotional longing for the readers. The two poets Kamala Das and Toru Dutt express their past memories in their writings. Poets or speakers recall their memories and express their emotions through poetry. In "A Hot Noon in Malabar" Kamala Das expresses her past memories with her parents in Malabar. In "Our Casuarina Tree", Toru Dutt expresses her past spending with her siblings.

In the poem "A Hot Noon in Malabar", Kamala Das discusses the event of crossing strangers in her house. Some beggars came, and they cried and explained their situation behind their begging. After that, a man came from the hill with a parrot in a cage, and he told astrology with the help of fortune cards. But the poet didn't believe it. When the Kuruva girls came, they looked like brown women, and they foretold the future by reading the palm. The Bangle-Sellers visited the poet's house. They contained different colours of bangles, like blue, red, and green. The bangle-seller used to spend time on the black floor that is road full of dust. They arrived at the poet's house at noon, after a long day of travelling in hot summer on a dusty road.

In "Our Casuarina Tree", Toru Dutt reminisces her past memories of her brother and sister. The poet's sister and brother died, and she missed her brother and sister. Her eyes filled with tears and recaptured the memories of her brother and sister. The poet watched outside through the window of her house. The Casuarina tree looked like a huge python. The tree seemed so strong. The flowers of the tree were huge in crimson clusters. The poet believed that the casuarina tree was heaven for birds and insects. At night, sounds from the tree made listeners relax with the bird singing. The poet watched the grey baboon and its offspring. The grey baboon sat on its branches watching the sunrise; the offspring sat on the lower branches playing. The kokilas began to creep that day with their sound. The trees' shadow fell on the huge tank. The poet said that she had spent her happy times under the Casuarina tree with her siblings and that reminiscence brought her happiness and longing for it.

In both the poems, the poets' feelings about their past memories made them smileand long for them. It gave them peace of mind and allowed them to reflect on and remember the best times of their lives. These two poems give readers pleasure and induce them to recollect their past memories.

Reference

Das, Kamala. "A Hot Noon in Malabar", *Summer in Calcutta*. Kottayam, D C Books, 2004.

Dutt, Toru. "Our Casuarina Tree." https://allpoetry.com/Our-Casuarina-Tree, retrieved, July 24, 2022.

Dutt, Toru. "Our Casuarina Tree." *Indian Literature*, vol. 9, no. 2, 1966, pp. 31–33.

CHAPTER SEVEN

Robots - A Humanoid Replica to Critique and Define the Essence of Humanity in Philip K. Dick's "Do Androids Dream of Electric Sheep?"

S. Beghin Bose,
Ph.D Research Scholar,

N ASHARUDEEN

Department of Computer Science,
S.T. Hindu College (Affiliated to M.S. University),
Kottar.

Science fiction covers stories about science and technology related with future. It is significant to identify that science fiction has a connection with the ideologies of science and the narration of these stories involve with fictitious laws and theories related with science. The plot in these fictions creates situations that are different from both the present day settings and the past. Science fiction comprises human elements, effects of new discoveries and the causes and outcome of scientific developments that may outcome in future. The settings of Science fiction are future, space, a changed world, and different universe. Early forerunners of science fiction are H. G. Wells and Jules Verne. Some well-known 20th century science fiction writings include *1984* by George Orwell, *Brave New World* by Alduous Huxley, and *The Fountainhead* by Ayn Rand. The four notable and well-recognized 20th century authors are Isaac Asimov, Arthur C. Clarke, Ray Bradbury, and Robert Heinlein.

Adam Roberts in *The History of Science Fiction* pinpoints the origin of science fiction based on the ancient Greek novel *Of Travel*. Science and adventure are linked together in Greek novels. Roberts examines this mode of link to be vanished for about two thousand years and then it had its next major appearance in16th century Europe.

According to Sawyer and Wright, the emergence of science fiction can be seen due to the rise of the utopian genre. Thomas More's *Utopia* (1516), the first utopian fictional text was written with a designed man's sensible dynamisms to objectify a better world. Brian W Aldiss and David Wingrove's history of science fiction titled *Trillion Year Spree: The History of Science Fiction* (1988) traces the origins of science fiction in the mutable atmosphere of an Industrial revolution that paved the way to the birth of Gothic fiction. Aldiss and Wingrove are identified with genre of gothic. Mary Shelley's *Frankenstein* (1818) reflects the original form of narration with the mode of science fiction that has developed.

The importance of H.G. Wells' scientific romances through his writings like *The Time Machine* and *The War of the Worlds.* John Reider, in his book *Colonialism and the Emergence of Science Fiction* (2008), argues that colonialism to be a science fiction "genre's texture, a persistent, important component of its displaced references to history, its engagement in ideological production, and its construction of the possible and the imaginable" (15). Patricia Kerslake also stated that the main subject matter of science fiction is "the theme of empire" (191). This theme of science fiction resulted with the rise and growth of science fiction. World Wars encountered with the devastating violence through catastrophes are reflected in Aldous Huxley's *Brave New World*– a proto-science fiction and George Orwell's *Nineteen Eighty –Four*. The themes of science and technology should have some impact on our everyday life. Hugo Gernsback first started his science fiction magazine, issued inexpensive periodicals like *Amazing Stories, Gernsback's Scientification*' magazine related with didactic story of miraculous future technology. This led a way to emerge of the leading science fiction practitioners like Isaac Asimov, Robert Heinlein and others. By 1930s, Gernsback's pulp magazines provided a way to other magazines along with Astounding Stories. John W Campbell edited the magazine and re-titled it as- *Astounding Science Fiction* and it emerged by adding scientific laws and it never loosed its grips over character expansion and ethical evenness. The 1960's saw the re-entry of British science fiction with Michael Moorcock as the editor of the magazine *New Worlds*. Thus it gave rise to the modern science fiction is Adam Roberts gave a comprehensive description of three types of science fiction. They are space travel science fiction in which the novel centres with moving to other planets, strange new climes; time travel science fiction based on both related to past and future and the third one is technology-oriented science fiction, a form prevailing in the 20th century.

Robots are a mainstay element in science fiction for nearly more than a hundred years. The term 'robot' was coined in a 1920 play *Rossum's Universal Robots* by Karel Capek, a Czech writer. The word 'robot' finds its origin in the Czech phrase 'robota', which means forced labour or servitude. Even the origin of the word 'robot' declares their role in science fiction. All through the science fiction genre, robots are controlled by their humanoid creators. Robots are built and programmed to fulfil certain roles or task. Their origin in the genre is linked to the Industrial Revolution, which saw a change from human labour to machine manufacturing.

The study indents to highlight the role of Robots -A Humanoid replica created by man to critique and define the essence of humanity. In is aimedto reflect the use of robots in literature as well as in the modern technology oriented world with reference to the novel *Do Androids Dream of Electric Sheep? by*Philip Kindred Dick. In 1872, Samuel Butler published an anonymous novel named *Erewhon*. It is the first text concerned with the rise of artificial intelligence. In *Runaround*, Asimov recommends a set of three rules that can be used to control robots. These rules are not like directions that govern humans and they are the rules rooted in programming and can prevent robots from causing harm to humans. These rules were established to safeguard humans when they are interacting with robots. The three laws are as follows:

1. A robot may not injure a human being or, through inaction, allow a human being to come to harm.

2. A robot must obey the orders given to it by human beings except where such orders would conflict with the First Law.

3. A robot must protect its own existence as long as such protection does not conflict with the First or Second Laws.

These laws were further advanced by Asimov and other writers over the years.

Robots are interesting both in real and fictional. Robots in science fiction are mainly a comeback to the Industrial Revolution and the ever mechanically evolving society we live in Philip Kindred Dick, an American science fiction writer, wrote 44 novels and about 121 short stories that appeared in science fiction magazines during his lifetime. The post-apocalyptic novel, *Do Androids Dream of Electric Sheep?* is the story of a distracted society due to the atomic war that resulted with the death of people and the elimination of different animal species. The remaining population's well-being is vulnerable by radioactive dust, and the humans who are previously affected by it are known as chicken heads. The non-affected are motivated to emigrate to Mars, so that they can stay safe while they are delivered with android servants as elevations. The new generation of the androids act in a rebellious way against their human masters, as a result they killed them and escaped to Earth.

Dick's novel confirms the various difficulties and manifested those difficulties with the form of human's alter ego, the android. Dick's androids by no means experience reproductive independence or a state of personhood for their membership into society. With limited exemptions the androids are mainly regarded as a hazard throughout the novel, thus Dick continuously warns humans about technological dangers. Dick highlights the struggles of the androids' based on the progeny defeat and a limited lifespan suggests that the android is a symbolic representation of his desire to re-examine the permanence of the androids in a post-human world and thus questions the supposed benefits of scientific development and its effects on humanity.

Philip K. Dick's novel *Do Androids Dream of Electric Sheep?* (1968), is set on post-apocalyptic Earth in the Bay Area of California. World War Terminus has overwhelmed the inhabitants of Earth and left it almost dilapidated, uninhabited and it resulted in forcing the survivors to migrate to Mars or to one of the other unnamed colony planets. As encouragement, the emigrants are given free android servants to attend them on their voyage and serve them on Mars. The androids are tremendously classy and vague from human beings.

They spend time with other humans and have jobs in order to feel more human, like J.R. Isidore does: "You have to be with other people, he thought. In order to live at all" (178).

In the novel, Rick Deckard is a bounty hunter who retires the rebellious androids. He lives with his wife, Iran, in an apartment in San Francisco and cannot live in Earth because of his job. They enjoy a Penfield mood organ that helps them to overcome dejection and sadness, also an electric sheep but they wish for a real and genuine real animal. Iran is a follower of Mercerism, a religion that is conducted by Wilbur Mercer. The followers of Mercerism use empathy boxes to fuse with Mercer who is climbing a hill, and thus they share a shared experience with empathy. To detect and cleanse the androids, Rick uses Voigt-Kampff test that examines them based on their empathic reactions and responses. Rick meets Rachael Rosen in the Rosen Association, which is a company that produces Nexus-6 androids. The company's executer wants to continue the androids production and tries to bribe Rick with expensive animals, but Rick never accepts his offers. Because of the disintegration, people are divided into the two groups of the normal and the chicken head. John Isidore is a chicken head who is not allowed to emigrate, and he works in artificial animals repair shop. He by mistake thinks a real cat to be an electric one and thus causes the death of the animal. He meets some of the fugitive androids in his apartment and communicates with them.

Isidore, as well as the whole population, is watching the most famous TV show, Buster Friendly and his friendly friends, is broadcasted twenty three hours a day. In searching for the androids, Rick inspects an opera singer, Luba Luft, who blames Rick and calls the police. Rick does not have any information about that police station and he finds out that it was under the control of the androids. After retiring inspector Garland, who is an android, Rick leaves the office with Phil Resch, another bounty hunter. Rick and Resch doubt that they may be androids; Resch goes through empathy test, and they make sure they are not androids. Then, Resch murders Luba Luft, and Rick wishes to retire from bounty hunting. Rick buys a real goat with the money from bounty hunting and decides to retire. When his boss asks him to retire three more androids, he calls Rachael Rosen for help, he tells her that if she were a human, he would love to marry her and stay with her. The intercourse with the android is another trick of the Rosen Association to prevent him from hunting the androids. He does not retire Rachael, but it does not change his decision in killing the other androids.

Although the androids in the novel do not grow up like humans, they have memories, but these memories are not real, whereas the memories of humans are real: "Only androids show up with false memory systems, it´s been found ineffective in humans" (110).

The novel discovers the moral inferences of enslaving a human-like organic machine, by depicting the uses in which the invention of a humanoid replica to evaluate and describe the essence of humanity. The essential aspects of humanity lied based on the qualities that distinguish humans from androids. Bounty hunters are employed by the remaining police agencies to protect the small communities of humans. They are the one who refuses to emigrate and are prevented from emigrating. It is due to the deteriorating effects of living in a radioactive environment with lowered IQs.

Bhabha states that the androids in the novel are constructed the way they look like real human beings, but they are actually not. Nevertheless, they want to be like humans: "It is the desire for a reformed, recognizable other, as a subject of a difference that is almost the same, but not quite, which is to say that the discourse of mimicry is constructed around an ambivalence" (86).

The novel surveys the psychology of the bounty hunter Rick Deckard as he retires escaped androids. Dick's novel reflects the peak of technological achievement as the android. The android is an organic robot that is aimed to be as human-like as probable in terms of both its physical appearance and behaviour. As the technology influenced, the android brain becomes more and more advanced, android behaviour mimics human behaviour and it resulted with a notion that android cannot be distinguished from a human form. Dick's narrator says that the androids were first invented as "Synthetic Freedom Fighters" for the use in World War Terminus, but later "had been modified to become the mobile donkey engine of the colonization program" (16). Based on this concept androids were originally created as a product of warfare and intended as spare soldiers, as a distinctive scenario for the human creation of technology.

The characters in Philip K. Dick´s novel *Do Androids Dream of Electric Sheep?* are may be humans or androids, since they are created as androids that are inferior to human beings and among the humans there are bounty hunters . They have the task to kill the android. Thus the androids intend to behave like human beings in their own way.

Earth's environment has become so hostile to human life that just by venturing out of doors people really impaired biologically that they are no longer considered human, but considered that they are to be a human subspecies. The social phase of human life resulted with a defining link between androids and humans. The novel suggests that while humans have compassion and empathy for all living things, androids are fully logical entities thus can only simulate empathy. Androids can be programmed to simulate instinctual emotional response that requires an interruption in a fraction of a second to yield with the simulation of empathy.

The novel thus explores the psychology of the alienated humans and their loneliness to signifying that at a biological level they struggle hard to be get a membership and identity in the human community and finally it ends with a feel of being alone. The absurdity about the human condition that the novel challenges is that humans can feel barred from the human community even in the presence of other humans. Another major theme of the novel is that human scuffle against futility, which is more usually a human desire to earmark a purpose to life in being an existent of reality.To sum up, Dick's multifaceted portrayal of the androids exemplifies the challenging nature of technology and the unpredictability that occurs with scientific inventions. The novel portrays different forms of subjectivity to depict the expansion of human faculties. The modern world is a world that is filled with human intelligence and artificial intelligence, and both become the result that occurred because of human himself. Thus in the novel, Technology acts as the nova to measure the invasion of earth by andys from Mars, transformation of human bodies by inducing technological manipulation and media power on earth. As a result it ended as a form of alarming digital junk and most important of all the humans' struggle to be humane in this humanoid world. His depiction exposes dehumanization that resulted from inaccurate class distinction that stems from questions of beginning, emotional response, and biological acceptability.

Reference

Dick, Philip K. *Do Androids Dream of Electric Sheep?*. London: Gollancz, 2011.

Hartwell, David G. Hard Science Fiction.*The Ascent of Wonder: The Evolution of Hard Science Fiction*. Ed. Hartwell and Kathryn Cramer. New York: TOR Books,1994.p 30–40.

Heidegger, Martin. *The Question Concerning Technology and Other Essays*. 1954. Trans. William Lovitt. New York: Harper Colophon, 1977.

Kerslake, Patricia. *Science Fiction and Empire*. Liverpool: Liverpool UP, 2007. Print.

Reider, John. *Colonialism and the Emergence of Science Fiction*. Middletown: Wesleyan UP, 2008.

Roberts, Adam. *The History of Science Fiction*. Hampshire: Palgrave Macmillan, 2006. Print.

Russ, Joanna. *Towards an Aesthetic of Science Fiction*. Science fiction Studies. 2.2 (1975): 112-19. JSTOR. Web. 24 Aug. 2015.

Sawyer, Andy and Peter Wright, eds. *Teaching Science Fiction*. London: Palgrave Macmillan, 2011.

Seed, David, ed. *A Companion to Science Fiction*. Malden: Blackwell Publishing, 2005

Sims, A. Christopher. *The Dangers of Individualism and the Human Relationship to Technology in Philip K. Dick'sDo Androids Dream of Electric Sheep?*. Science Fiction Studies; V(36)1.2019.

Wolk, Anthony. *The Swiss Connection: Psychological Systems in the Novels of Philip K. Dick. Philip K. Dick: Contemporary Critical Interpretations.* Ed. Samuel J. Umland. Westport, CT: Greenwood, 1995. 101-26.

CHAPTER EIGHT

Longing for Identity in Shashi Deshpande's "The Dark Holds No Terrors"

T. Deepalakshmi,
Assistant Professor,
Department of English,
Edayathangudy G. S. Pillay Arts and Science College (Autonomous),
Nagapattinam.

The male domination of a woman's life is a natural phenomenon in a patriarchal society, and the consequent relegation of a woman to a secondary position seems to have prompted Indian women writers to take up the cause of women. This paper stressed the need for women to break free from the shackles of their traditional position and see their own need for self-fulfilment as more important than the duty of sacrificing themselves for their husbands and children.

The novel *The Dark Holds No Terrors* by Shashi Deshpande basically expresses the frustration and disappointment of women who experience social and cultural oppression in a male-dominated society. It highlights the agony and trauma experienced by women in a male-dominated and tradition bound society. They bring out the absurdity of rituals and customs, which, help to perpetuate the myth of male superiority. This clearly points out, how a woman grows from self-surrender to assert her individuality with a newly emerged identity. A father and daughter (Patriarchal family) Relationship:

In their daughter's life, the father's personality is crucial. Typically, a daughter's first male-female relationship is with her father. However, it is clear from the start of this book, The Dark Holds No Terror, that the protagonist, Sarita, and her father are unable to communicate effectively. She truly comes back because she can no longer tolerate her husband's sexual sadism. But she was unable to communicate her emotions or anguish to her father. Like an unhappy host welcoming an unwanted guest, the father is uncaring and not supportive enough.

- Like a tradition Indian father, he enjoys the privilege of being the Master and head of the family. As we know from Sarita, he is not concerned with the problems of his own family members. He had always been so much a man, the Master of the house, not to be bothered by any of the trivial of daily routine. (*The Dark Holds No Terrors,* 20).

In Indian society, married women are not supposed to return to their parental house without their husband or have any quarrels or divorce. They were supposed to stay in the house with her husband till his death. So, when Sarita's father finds her standing alone with the suitcase, he frowns and knits his eyebrows like any other typical Indian father. Also, when Sarita tells her father about her husband, who tortures her sexually, it is something beyond the understanding of her father, who always maintained distance and reserve with his wife. Thus, the root of these problems also seems to lie in social attitudes.

When a mother and daughter relationship is born in a household, she is considered a debt, a liability; whereas when a boy is born, he is considered an asset, who will earn and care for his parents later on. Any expenditure for a boy does not seem much, but when it comes to girls, there is always the thought at the back of their minds that they have to pay a huge sum of money as dowry for the girl. They are considered a burden, to be married off at great expense-even now, many parents start saving money for their daughter's marriage from the time she is born. This novel basically discusses the blatant gender discrimination shown by parents towards their daughters and their desire to have a male child. Sarita's unhappiness is a major factor in the Hindu tradition. It is a well-known fact that a Hindu values a son over a daughter.

At large, mothers share a very strange and complex relationship with their daughters. Typically, mothers want their daughters to adhere to traditions and codes. They think it's a traditional bound life, which would keep their daughter safe. But, sometimes, the mother can also be found cruel and hostile towards her own daughter, treating her with a sense of rivalry. The hostile chauvinistic societal environment has moulded the psyche of a mother as a woman and also made the young uninitiated child a special object of the mother's persecution. This novel exhibits the trauma of a girl child who has suffered the bullying and curtailment of activity by her mother. The girl-child Saru grows up as a victim of her mother's sexist and gender-based bias; which further reduces her later life into a desperate struggle.

For instance, it is found that the mother has expressed her anguish and the gender-bias through the natural element, sunlight, which she feels is a barrier to women's beauty or to their fair complexion. Right from the beginning, Sarita is made to understand that she is a girl and she is inferior to her brother, in every way. The sole purpose of a woman's existence is to please her man. She has just remained a thing to be passed on from parents to husband.

As for her behavior, she always kept two different measuring yards, one for the son and the other for the daughter.

In this way, a traditional mother thinks that it is their duty to remind their daughter that she is a girl and she should behave accordingly. The socio-cultural conditioning of a girl is still a part of Indian culture. Hence, Saru's lively, full of life, is gradually suffocated by her mother's constant criticism and fault finding. Saru is always made to feel ugly, unwanted, and undesirable. "I was an ugly girl, At least, my mother told' me so". (*The Dark Holds No Terrors, 61)*.

The mother-daughter relationship in this novel is based on gender-bias and loveliness. Usually, mothers serve as role models for their daughters. They provide examples of how to be an individual, a mother, and a wife. In this novel, Sarita is deprived of motherly love, care, and affection. She is just treated as a playmate and governess for her brother, Dhurva. She is always ignored and neglected in favour of her brother. She is not given much importance. Later, it is found that Sarita rejects her mother and also the meaningless rituals, like circumambulating the tulsi plant. "The tulsi had been the only spot of green. But that had gone as well...." *(The Dark Holds No Terrors,* 1).

In the Indian context, circumambulating the tulsi plant by a woman is meant to increase the life span of husbands. Here, Sarita rejects these rituals. This rejection indicates her freedom or individuality and her capability to see her life independently of her mother or past. The Protagonist, Sarita, as a Mother, Sarita wishes not to be like her mother. She is not only a wife and a mother of two children, but also a successful lady doctor. In reality, the working housewife is doubly burdened with duties and conjugal relations both at home and at work. By chance, the balance is not maintained well, and then the feelings of disenchantment and imbalance lead to separation, and all the relations are uprooted, making it a psychological problem.

Sarita's life has turned out to be a problematic one. As a doctor, she is successful and becomes quite busy, which ultimately upsets her family life. The aspect of the doctor in her is more often seen than that of the wife, and the mother in her. So, as a wife and a mother, she is unable to devote her time to her husband and children's needs. Hence, she fails first as a wife and secondly as a mother. She finds herself placed at her personal level; she feels the gradual disappearance of love and family attachment. Renu, her daughter in this novel, is often portrayed as cold, silent, a woman despite her age, and so on. As a mother, she sometimes fails to understand her daughter's odd behaviour. It is also observed that Renu does not talk much, even to her mother, as children her age do.

- "Renu what is the matter?
- They are used to being without me. I'm out most of the day, anyway. And I told you about my JanakiBai. As long as she's with them, I didn't have to worry‖. (*The Dark Holds No Terrors,* 71).

She appointed Janakibai to look after her children. But, they still long for motherly love and care. This also shows the city life, where most parents appoint a maid to look after their children. But it is a well-known fact that nobody can replace the place of the mother in the family. There are many instances which clearly show their longings for motherly love and care.

Sarita once discovered her daughter, Renu, drawing a picture with black crayons. It is like a deep, dark forest. The trees are almost tall and straight. On looking at her drawing, Sarita feels that, unlike other children, Renu draws not a colourful picture but a dark one. Thus, the child's psychology is shown or expressed through the picture. The children of Renu's age usually draw only colourful pictures, but Renu draws a frightful one.

This picture can be inferred in different ways. On the one hand, the child in the picture may be considered as Renu. Through her drawing, she reflected her loneliness or uncaring child's attitude, longing for her mother's love. So this picture clearly shows her mind or sense of loneliness. This kind of utter loneliness a human being faces in life stands as the core of *The Dark Holds No Terrors.*

Sarita marries Manohar, against the will of her parents. She is a wife who is more successful than her husband. This is the main cause of her sufferings and physical torture. This change or reversal of social status shatters Sarita's life into pieces. She is independent and a woman in the outside world, but inside she doesn't know how to deal with her husband's sexual torture. Thus, it clearly shows that the family institution begins to disintegrate when a woman achieves greater economic or social status than a man. The problem faced by Sarita is the problem of many learned and professional women in society. It is known that Indian society is still bound by tradition and superstition. No one dares challenge the existing male-dominant order.

After marriage, Saru becomes a successful and recognised lady doctor. She begins to enjoy superior financial and social status with the help of an outsider, Boozie. This creates an inferiority complex in Manohar and he becomes a sadist who gets pleasure from insulting his wife, harassing and hurting her sexually. Saru cannot object at first because her mother had moulded her psyche to accept the pains and sufferings in order for her marriage to be successful. She decides to keep her marriage in favour of her husband. But Manohar's disgusting behaviour in the night frightened and trapped her like an animal. In all these acts, she finds herself lonely and a dissatisfied person. The isolation and fragmentation in her marital life make Saru look for other possibilities. Boozie, her mentor, takes a personal interest in her, not engaging in any physical relationship. Never, she has looked for love beyond marriage.

Her affairs with Boozie and Padmakar Rao are temporary substitutes for her unfulfilled marital life. She is not ready to live in a dingy two-room flat in a suburban area all her life. She wishes to have a house of her own. She also wants to live a comfortable life. So she uses Boozie as support to elevate her career. According to Saru, Boozie is a handsome, masterful man. Everything about him, right from his language, his skills, appears to Saru, in perfect management.

She reveals that her other extramarital partner is Padmakar, also known as Padma, a student from medical school whom she meets after graduation and becomes a doctor. After a few incidences, Padmakar discourages Saru from developing a closer bond with her because she wants to put a stop to their connection. She is not being comforted or soothed by this relationship. With regard to love or passion, she says

- And I? Now, I knew it was not just the consequence I feared and hated, but also the thing itself. When had I imagined? Love? Romance? Both, I knew too well were illusions, and not Relevant to my life any way. And the code word of our age is neither love nor romance, but sex. Fulfillment and happiness came, not through love Alone but sex. And for me sex was now a dirty word. (*The Dark Holds No Terrors,* 133).

In a way, these two men in the life of Saru prove that their relationship gives no solace; it is only a disillusioned relationship. She is disgusted with the behaviour of her husband, and as a dissatisfied person, she deserts her husband and children and goes to her parental home under the pretext of her mother's death.

These relationships in Sarita's life help her to tackle her problems. She feels that she has done injustice to her mother, husband, children, and everybody else. She takes this opportunity to examine, to begin, and to reinforce her indispensability. She is also able to think sensibly and logically. She realises that she has to accept everything with her daughter, sister, and wife as they are. She understands that escaping is not a permanent solution to the problems, but it has to come from within.

Reference

Deshpande, Shashi. *The Dark Holds No Terrors*. New Delhi: Vikas, 1980.

CHAPTER NINE

"The Verger": A Prosperous Businessman

A. Durgadevi,
MA English (2020-2022),
Edayathangudy G. S. Pillay Arts & Science College
(Autonomous),
Nagapattinam.

William Somerset Maugham was born on January 25, 1874 in Paris and died on December 16, 1965 in Nice, France. His famous works are Liza of Lambeth (1897), Orientations (1898), and The book bag (1932). He was reputedly the highest paid writer during the 1930's. He was a qualified physician but gave it up it to write full time. His short stories had human follies and foibles. He should have great understanding and tolerance in depicting the ironies of life. He was one of the most significant travel writers of the inter-war years. The Somerset Maugham Award is a British literary prize given each year by the Society of authors. Set up by William Somerset Maugham in 1947, the awards enable young writers to enrich their work by gaining experience in foreign countries.

"The Verger" is an excellent short story by William Somerset Maugham. In this tale, A.E. Foreman is a verger in the church.

He is illiterate. When the church has a new bishop, the vicar is sent away. He has no confidence in himself to learn at his old age. So he starts a business. In the turn of events, he becomes a successful businessman. Here, Maugham writes that education does not always play a significant role in the progress of men. He was very proud of his profession. He was very happy to wear the verger's gown during the funeral and wedding ceremonies. He had been verger of the church for sixteen years. He thought that the verger's gown was a dignified symbol of his office. Though illiterate, it never interfered with his work.

The new vicar of St. Peter's church was astonished to learn that the long-serving verger was an uneducated man. He gave Foreman three months to educate himself. But Foreman said that he did not want to start learning how to read and write at his old-age. And he was ready to leave the church when a new verger was found.

Foreman was very distressed and so he went on the wrong route towards home. He was tired and wanted to smoke but found no cigarette shop. So, he decided to open a shop to sell cigarettes and cakes. Over the next decade, he started up more and more shops. He soon became a wealthy man in the process of depositing his profits at the bank.

The manager of the bank where Foreman had deposited his earnings told him to invest money in guilt-edged securities. He submitted the details of broking stocks and shares. He asked Foreman to read the conditions before signing the papers. Foreman confessed that he was illiterate and could read and write only his name. The stunned manager asked him what he would have been if he had been educated. Foreman replied gently that he would be a verger at St. Peter's church.

The irony of the story is that if Foreman had been educated, he would have been a poor verger in St. Peter's church doing errand jobs. But without proper education, and still remaining illiterate, the verger had now become a prosperous businessman. It is interesting how intelligence is little more than a short foot-rule by which one measures the infinite achievements of circumstances. It is a simple tale about a simple man who did his duties with great joy and dedication. Maugham explains that one's weaknesses never limit his success.

Reference

http://www.sinden.org/verger.html

CHAPTER TEN

METAMORPHOSIS IN "PYGMALION" BY GEORGE BERNARD SHAW

R. Indhu,
I - B.Ed.St. Xavier College of Education, Kumbakonam
G. Dharani, BA English (2018-2021),
Swami Dayananda College of Arts & Science, Manjakkudi.

Shaw became a socialist after reading Karl Marx's Das Capital and later joined the "Fabian Society." With the help of William Archer, Shaw became the reviewer of books for The Pall Mall Gazette and pictures for "The World". He started writing for the evening paper, *The Star*. He died at the age of 95. His famous plays are *Caesar and Cleopatra, Man and Superman, Pygmalion, St. Joan, The Apple Cart, Back to Methuselah,* and *Androcles and the Lion.* His play *St. Joan* was made into a movie in 1957. His play *Pygmalion* was made into a movie, The First *Pygmalion.* The movie won him an Academy Award for the best adapted screenplay. The play was also made into a musical called *My Fair Lady.*

This play, *Pygmalion*, belongs to the 'Irish Literature'. Irish literature is one of the oldest literatures in Europe. The writings which are in Irish, Latin, and English come under the heading of Irish Literature. In the thirteenth century, there was the introduction of the English language in Ireland. A rapid displacement of the Irish language by English took place in the latter part of the seventeenth century. Most of the works of high quality were in the Irish language, even though English was the dominant literary language in Ireland. There were a number of well-known Irish authors in English in the 21st century. In his play Pygmalion, George Bernard Shaw attacks the relations between the classes of the Victorian era.

The name Pygmalion is a boy's name, which is a legendary sculptor in Greek mythology, who fell in love with a statue of a beautiful woman which he carved from ivory. There have been many adaptations of the story *Pygmalion,* including notable plays by Jean Jacques Rousseau and George Bernard Shaw. The symbolism in the play has to do with Henry Higgins's love for his own creation. The play, *Pygmalion,* is a reworking of the Greek myth of Pygmalion and Galatea Aphrodite, the goddess of love and beauty, transformed the ivory statue into an actual woman, Galatea, by breathing life into her. *Pygmalion* and Galatea got married and lived happily ever after. A great change in appearance or character is called a "metamorphosis." It is the process of great and usually rather sudden changes in form and habits. Metamorphosis, or transformation, is one of the themes in *Pygmalion.* It is a play of five acts, not in scenes. Each act represents the transformation of the central character, "Eliza Doolittle." The conversation between Professor Higgins and Colonel Pickering emerged as the best bet. At the beginning of the play, Eliza speaks the Cockney dialect with 'Freddy'. But at last, she is able to speak English like a duchess. Dialect plays a crucial role in the play. The simple flower girl, Eliza, transforms into a pretty girl like a duchess. Not only Eliza, but also her father, Alfred Doolittle, has transformed in the story. He was a garbage man at the beginning of the play. But at last, he became a millionaire. The play, *Pygmalion,* transforms "Mythical Play" into "Victorian Romance." This story expresses the line that

'Dirty Changed into Beauty'. The metamorphosis of this play starts with the transformation of Eliza's clothes (costumes). The transformation of her clothes made her father, Alfred Doolittle, fail to recognise his own daughter. Thus the metamorphosis proves the importance of outer appearances. At the beginning of the play, Eliza speaks the following dialogue with her cockney slang; "Nah then, Freddy: look wh'y' growing, death "There's manners f' yer! Te – oo banches o voylets trod into the mad."(Pygmalion 2-3)

The transformation of Eliza was gradually increased. This transformation has effects on other characters also. At first, Eliza has a great impact on Professor Higgins. He is an expert in phonetics. He is a great teacher but has no human feelings and does not understand others' feelings. Eliza was deeply attached to Higgins. He ignores her feelings. Even he doesn't consider her a girl. But at last, Higgins feels the vacuum in his heart and he is terribly upset. This is the transformation from his inner side. Through his transformation, it is known that Higgins is kind-hearted and concerned for Eliza. Alfred Doolittle, Eliza's father, is self-confident, but he is uneducated and immortal, often giving to drinking and debauchery. His appearance was completely vigorous. Because he is Garbage man and then becomes rich and dresses like a fine gentle man. He delivers lectures and becomes the most original moralist in England. It shows how he has modified his character and outer appearance perfectly. Actually, Alfred Doolittle was a bachelor. Eliza was his illegitimate daughter. His middle class morality compels him to marry his sixth mistress. He is changed by wealth at the end of the story. He wants a little money, so he asks for money. But now his role is reversed, and people are trying to charm him for money or favours. Freddy's transformation into a teenager marked a turning point in the story. In the beginning, though he was rich, his mother didn't give him an adequate education. His mother wants him to become a personal secretary. But he doesn't have such an idea. His mother always calls him helpless. His sister says that he has no common sense. He hasn't done anything noteworthy in his life. He is ineffectual and unworkable. His life was the biggest question mark. His mother worried about his life and how he would lead his life. But when he meets Eliza, he has completely transformed. Freddy's transformation is the indispensable one. The theme of metamorphosis is put forth here. Love is the foundation for the transformation of characters. Love is a powerful weapon that can completely transform a person who falls deeply in love. The changes may be valid or invalid. It depends on individuals. Freddy's true love for Eliza transforms him from an impractical to a fruitful character. That's why the subtitle of the play is called "A Romance in Five Acts".

Eliza was a kind and innocent girl in the play. But Higgins changed her in all aspects. He changed her clothes, her manners, her confidence level, and her diction.But at the end of the play, Eliza makes a change in Higgins' heart when he realises that she is leaving. Higgins used her as a tool to enhance his reputation in society.

Eliza's transformation is more profound. Shaw used this to show the "positives" and "negatives." On the positive side, Eliza has built her sense of confidence and self-worth. She revolts and declares herself against the verbal abuse of Higgins, such as his calling her a "Squashed Cabbage". Henry treats her as a thing, but Eliza insists, at the end, on being treated as a girl.On the negative hand, however, the play indicates that by transforming Eliza into a lady like a duchess, Higgins has left her unfit for any role in society. She could earn enough to meet her own needs even though she was a poor flower seller. As a lady, she must marry and rely on a man for support, as working in the class would be inappropriate for a woman.

Eliza appears filthy. Her clothes are in need of washing and her teeth are in need of a dentist. She wore a soot-covered hat, tacky and irritated clothing. Her boots are much the worse to wear. These are things that express that she is from a lower class. Why does she appear like this? Because her earning money was enough for her food only, she didn't have adequate money for her needs. Her cockney accent and unschooled vocabulary, as well as her outward appearance, label her as lower class.It is her “Kerbstone” English. In the Victorian period, women were represented as fragile and helpless, as women were physically weaker than men. So, they always need protection from men and their help. Why do we say this? In the first part, Eliza was like that. She is uneducated and always needs help from her father. But it becomes futile.

At the last part, Eliza completely changed her speaking style, manners, behaviors, and dressing style. She transformed Kerbstone Flower Girl with deplorable English into a regal figure fit to consort with nobility. The hostess was much impressed by Eliza's beauty, graceful style, and accent in her speech at the ambassador's party. The Higgins student praised her, saying she was like a foreign princess because no English lady could speak as well as she did. She transforms into an independent woman, a strong lady and capable of doing anything. She breaks the rules of the Victorian era. With the companionship of Freddy, Eliza lives a respectful and proud life. “But of course you are; you are never ill. So to see you again, Colonel Pickering. Quite chilly this morning, isn't it?"(Pygmalion 96).

The bet between Higgins and Colonel Pickering emerged as a “bet”. The bet kicked off the theme of metamorphosis in the character of the poor flower girl into a duchess. The Transformation is the concealed title for this play, *Pygmalion*. Shaw proves this in the dialect, outer appearances, personal life, and culture of every character in the play. It is a complex work of art by Shaw. Jane Rolland Martin said, “Eliza is nothing less than a whole person transformation.”

Reference

Kanwal.G.R. *English Literature Series*. Surjeet Publications, 2001.

CHAPTER ELEVEN

Analysis of Abilities and Disabilities of Melody in Sharon Draper's "Out of My Mind"

R. Karthikayini,
Language Trainer,
Training and Placement,
Edayathangudy G. S. Pillay Arts and Science College (Autonomous),
Nagapattinam.

Sharon M. Draper is an American children's writer. *Out of My Mind* is a novel that deals with the life of Melody Brooks, who is eleven and was born with cerebral palsy. She cannot walk and communicate with others, but she is an intellectual girl. She uses a wheelchair to move and depends on others for every action. She cannot do any work without the help of others. Even though her body has problems functioning, her mind is very sharp when compared to normal people. She has a unique capability of photographic memory. Her mind is like a camera, and she can observe all the things she sees. "Here's the thing: I'm ridiculously smart, and I'm pretty sure I have a Photographic memory. It's like I have a camera in my head, and if I see or hear something, I click it, and it says" (13). Melody used to watch a lot of informational television shows. No one can recognise her intelligence until she partakes in a programme.

Melody worries about her disability in speaking with others. She can hear her inner voice, but she never speaks out loudly. It seems that Melody wants to fight to fulfil her wishes. At the age of five, the doctor diagnosed her with cerebral palsy and suggested sending Melody to a nursing home. But her parents didn't do that, and they have decided to help Melody lead a normal life without worrying about her disability. Melody's mother sent her to an elementary school to acquire a basic education. She attended the class like a baby, learning the same things like the alphabet every day. Melody gets frustrated by this repetition because she is actually an intelligent girl, but she cannot speak or write, so she is unable to express herself to others. "By the time I was two, all my memories had words, and all my words had meanings. But only in my head. I have never spoken one single word" (2).

She compares herself with normal people and believes that normal people are not realising their blessings of continuous speaking and writing, which is really greater than all things in the world. She can realise the value of speaking and also know the importance of language. "Everybody uses the words to express themselves. Expect me. And I bet most people don't realise the real power of words. But I do" (8).

Mrs. V is a neighbour to Melody, and she is portrayed as an important person in Melody's life. She has taught her how to catch herself whenever she falls from her wheelchair. It helps Melody become self-sufficient. Melody's doctor suggests a medi-talker that helps her communicate with others. She gets a communication device, which makes her talk with other people, and it also leads her to participate in a whiz kid quiz programme.

In her school, a new teacher starts a programme for special-needs students. Melody gets an aide, Catherine, to help her. Melody faces many problems in her school. Bullies disturb her in school. Her friend Rose also sometimes does not understand her and also hurts her inner feelings. Melody faces many struggles in her life, both physically and mentally. Her disabilities are only noticed by others. She has many unique abilities compared to normal children, but she is unable to reveal her abilities to others. All the students in the school treat her like a loser. But nobody knows her talent or intelligence. Once, she gets a chance to prove her abilities to others. Her aide, Catherine, helps her to join the Whiz Kids Quiz Team, and Melody makes the team qualify for the next level. They get a chance to participate in a next level competition in Washington, D.C. She is very happy and eagerly waiting for the competition because she gets a chance to go to Washington, D.C. for free. She says, "I don't think they get paid very much, because they never stay very long, but they should get a million dollars." What they do is really hard, and I don't think most folks get that" (52).

Unfortunately, the flight was cancelled, but Melody's teammates had gone to Washington, D.C. by earlier flight. Melody is very upset because she is unable to participate in the competition. After getting into this unfortunate situation, she recalls the unforgettable, bitter incident that happened in the past. Melody has a little sister named Penny; she loves her sister very much. One day, she was unable to go to school when her mother's health was not good. On that day, her sister Penny, a small baby, slipped out of the house. Her mother did not recognise it. Melody tried to inform her mother by kicking, hitting, and screaming to warn her mother, but she failed to understand her. Penny slipped out of the house and fell down in the path of the car. Penny got injured heavily. Melody felt guilty about this incident. Although she saw her sister, she couldn't save her. "Maybe I'm not so different from everyone else after all" (293).

Finally, Melody realises her abilities and disabilities and believes that she cannot lead a normal life, even if she has a lot of intelligence when compared to others. She agrees with all the things that happen around her. Melody's teammates return to the class, and they apologise for leaving her. They got the ninth prize in the competition without the involvement of Melody. Melody forgives and laughs at them. She thinks about the value of her abilities and the next day, she starts writing her auto-biography with the help of Catherine.

This paper has analysed the abilities and disabilities of Melody Brooks, who is unable to explain her pains and struggles, but her talents are explored more when comparing other children. She cannot communicate with others but can communicate with herself with her mind. She can capture anything like a camera, and it stores all the memories in her lifetime. This is the life-lesson given by Draper to all aged people who get worried about their disabilities instead of recognising their abilities to run their lives in a prosperous way.

Reference

Draper, Sharon M. *Out of My Mind.* Athenaeum Books for Young Readers, 2013.

CHAPTER TWELVE

Eco – Critical Analysis in Walt Whitman's "Out of the Cradle Endlessly Rocking"

K. Kiruthika,
BA English (2019-2022),
Swami Dayananda College of Arts and Science,
Manjakkudi.

Walt Whitman was an American poet, essayist, and journalist. A humanist, he was a part of the transition between transcendentalism and realism. He was well known as the "Father of Free Verse". His collection of poetry was tasted in a book called Leaves of Grass. Whitman's "Out of the Cradle Endlessly Rocking" says something about the relationship between suffering and art. However, some critics see it as an elegy for his beloved.It was first published under the title "A Child's Reminiscence", but later it was renamed as, "A Word Out of the Sea," published in 1860. It was first published in 1871 under the title "Out of the Cradle Endlessly Rocking."The poem traces how a boy matures into a poet through his experiences of love and death. The poet recalls the he-bird and she-bird, as well as his own mournful expression from his youth. The poet was greatly captivated by nature, so he minutely observed the activities of nature and noticed them. The bird's singing is natural, but the poet matches it up with endless sea waves. The he-bird mourns for the missing she-bird, but it seems to be a complaint given by the he-bird to the poet. The young boy was influenced by the he-bird feeling. From the poet's point of view, the beautiful crescent moon looked like a swollen moon because it was also affected by the he-bird. The poet has good knowledge, but here he was stimulated to write more poems as much as he was influenced by the he-bird's song. It was natural to reminisce about the sad things and worry. Here the poet recollected his past (he-bird mourns) and cried like a child, how he suffered in his youthful days. The young child didn't know how to speak in a proper way, but in this poem he recreated the song of the he-bird.

Loving is universal. Gandhiji says that "Where there is love, there is life". Here the he-bird expresses how they love each other from dark to light, sun to moon. Life is full of twists and turns. This is not only for human life but it also happens in birds' lives too. Like that one fine day that she-bird missed out on the hot bed. Even after days, months, and years passed, she had not yet returned to the nest. The he-bird wandered here and there in search of his she-bird. Wind blowing is a natural thing, but in this poem, the he-bird requested it to blow strongly. How much can it reach? Because only the he-bird's song will be heard by the she-bird. The young boy wept for his brother's (he-bird) sorrow. The little boy has a feeling that has shrunk from mankind. The he-bird chewed his song, which was influenced by his brother. The young boy listened very carefully to He-bird's song because he wanted to translate the emotions of He-bird in the form of poetry to humans.

The poet fitly spelled out that the sea waves came one by one, seeming to console one another, but the he-bird longs for somebody to console him. He was deeply inspired by nature from this point of view, as it was clearly noted. The moon's rising and setting was a natural cycle, though it was sometimes delayed. But here the he-bird says that it was full of sorrow because there was a delay in its appearance. The sea waves touching the land are natural, but it seems to be a sign of love shown to it. The bird felt lonely while seeing those things happen around it. One dark night under a gloomy moon, the he-bird saw something. There was no light, so it considered it as his she-bird and started a loud voice. He now felt that he was alone, so he imagined something that was not real. How the young boy fails in his life and suffers greatly in order to forget everything that has happened to him, as the he-bird is now attempting.

He was in a mad love state, so everything he saw seemed to be his she-bird.The moon falling is natural, but the bird said that it was falling down because of an overload of pain. The sea wave's sound is so mild to hear, but here it acted as a messenger, and later it became a disturbance for him. At first, the sea wave's sound helped the he-bird search for a she-bird, but now it was very hard to hear for the he-bird. In the old days, ancestors used the birds to find directions. Likewise, here the he-bird gave dictation to the she-bird to come back to him and not to go somewhere else.

The young boy states that that nature is still that as same as it was before. But the he-bird's feelings were constant. The young boy realised that he was a born and nature plays a vital role in everyone's life. Nature revealed a poet who was hidden in a young boy. The he-bird sing for his she-bird but it seems to be lament to the young boy. Now he was become a poet so he imagines like that. The bird's song helped him to write many poems and he influenced by he-bird. The poet's knowledge is not up to the level that he learnt from the nature, his quest was unquenchable so he urges the bird to train him more and more that he needs the acquaintance of knowledge in abundance. The sea wave roaring is a nature, but the poet argues that it was saying something to him as much he was attracted by the nature. First he translated the bird's song and he was translating the sea waves sound that much he had gained knowledge from the nature. At last the wild sea waves changed to mild whisper waves and conferred him as a poet to him. That was clearly understood by him and finally raised as a poet.

Everyone's life has a birth and death it is nature. Henry Wade Beecher says that "Death is not an end. It is new impulsive". Death is quiet nature so accept it and move on. The poet learnt a very good lesson from the nature. Nature can create good things if humans are good; if humans are bad it turns as enemy to humans.

Reference

Bychowski, Gustav. "Walt Whitman: A Study in Sublimation." *Psychoanalysis and the Social Sciences*. Ed. Geza Roheim. New York: International Universities, 1950. 223-261.

Whitman, Walt. *Leaves of Grass: Comprehensive Reader's Edition.* Ed. Harold W. Blodgett and Sculley Bradley. New York: New York UP, 1965.

CHAPTER THIRTEEN

Hester Prynne as a Victim of Puritans - Woman Oppression in "The Scarlet Letter" by Nathaniel Hawthrone

K. Lawanya,
BA English (2019-2022),
Swami Dayananda College of Arts and Science,
Manjakkudi.

The title of the novel *The Scarlet Letter* indicates to the bright red color letter 'A'.It symbolizes the sin, shame and redemption of the whole story.

Kate Millet accuses Hawthorne of misogyny. One more critic says, in American literature women are consider as dangerous and morally inferior creatures when they are free and independent in their passion and in Hawthorne's The Scarlet Letter, the same image is shown. In Hawthorne's writings, as critics says, women are thought inferior. Though it was the mindset of that particular society but he raised idea of feminism in this novel. His themes in novels are dark and gloomy and that's why he is famous for dark romantic novels. In 1852, he published The Blithe dale Romance. It is his Big Romantic Novel.

The novel tells the story of the lady named Hester Prynne who conceives a daughter through an affair. This is more than the story of a woman. It is a portrait of the puritan period in American life. Though to us, the customs seem grim and the punishments hard. Normally some peoples enjoying others sufferings and spreading rumors about problems. In Boston puritans gathered often to watch criminals punished. Hester Prynne has got punishment to stand on the scaffold for three hours and to wear the scarlet letter "A" for the rest of her life.Oscar Wilde says, "I don't mind plain women being puritans. It is the only excuse they have for being plain."

From this it is understood that how terrible their punishment and people was? Many of the women in the crowd are angered by her beauty and quiet dignity also. They demand to tell her baby pearl's father name. They don't have rights to criticize or make fun of someone without knowing them properly. Hester is tall with a head of dark glossy hair and a beautiful face with deeply set black eyes. Hester looks out into the crowd she noticesRoger Chilling Worth, her husband. His face becomes horrified when he sees Hester on the scaffold. He quickly places his finger on his lips to silence her. He asks a man in the crowd about her and tells the story of his wife's adultery. No one there knows that Chilling Worth is Hester's husband. The stranger tells Hester's history. She has been marrying a scholar from England but had arrived in Massachusetts alone. She lives alone in Boston for two years before falling into sin. Chilling Worth ask who fathered Hester's child. The man says that is a mystery and suggests him that Hester's husband come from Europe to investigate the matter himself. To believe in the stranger's words are not right. He has to think about the right thing.

Mr. Wilson and the minister of Hester's church, Arthur Dimmesdale (pastor) question her but she refuse to name her lover. She returns from prison, Pearl cries uncontrollably. The prison guards allow a doctor in to help her. The jailer brings Chilling Worth, now a physician. Hester fears Chilling Worth has been poisoning her. Chilling Worth forgives Hester for betraying him. This is a good thing he hasn't shown his hatred her. He asks her to tell him the name of her lover but she refuses. She is afraid that her lover and his position will be affected in some way. Then Chilling Worth warns if she reveals him, he will destroy the child's father. Hester agrees to him and suspects she will regret it.

After three years, Hester now free from prison decides not to leave Boston. She settles in a cottage at the edge of town and earns with her needle work. She lives a quiet poor life with her daughter, Pearl. Hester's daughter troubles her and questions about the scarlet letter. Hester hearing rumors that she may lose Pearl. Hester goes to visit Governor Bellingham to enquire about these rumors and to deliver a pairs of gloves that she has made for him. John Wilson, Chilling Worth and Dimmesdale arrive at Governor Residence. The men tease Pearl calling her a Demon-Child because of her scarlet letter clothing but he stop when he realizes that she is Hester's daughter. No matter how much punishments has given the Governor asks Hester how she justify keeping pearl. Hester says she will teach pearl what she has learned from wearing the scarlet letter. The Governor says that the letter is her badge of shame. Mr. Wilson asks Pearl "who made her?" Pearl replays that she was plucked from the rosebush. Her childishness is evident by this answer. The governor alarmed by her response. Hester says that she will die before giving up Pearl and begs Dimmesdale to defend her. As a mother she suffers a lot here. Dimmesdale argues that Pearl has sent by god to serve as Hester's one true punishment and to guard from sinning again. His speech convinces the Governor not to take Pearl from Hester. That is actually great and also his duty.

Dimondale's health has worsened and he seems often with his hand over his heart. Chilling Worth treats Dimmesdale and being in such close contact with Dimmesdale because Chilling Worth suspects Dimmesdale that he was the father of Hester's child. He applies psychological pressure on Dimmesdale. One evening Dimmesdale is sleeping, Chilling Worth sees the symbol that represents his shame on his chest that gives him a joy.

Hester and Dimmesdale meet in the forest. He decides to flee Boston with Hester. Dimmesdale goes to the square where Hester was punished years earlier. Hester has shocked by Dimmesdale action. Several days later Hester meet again Dimmesdale and tells him of her husband and his desire for revenge. She convinces Dimmesdale to leave Boston in secret on a ship to Europe where they can start a new life. They want to live together. Inspired by this plan Dimmesdale seems to gain new energy. One Election Day, he climbs upon the scaffold and confesses his sin. Finally he has revealed the secrets and he has died in Hester's arms. Later the most witness a scarlet letter "A" upon his chest, although someone deny this statement.

Doris lee says, "Kindness Is the Best Form of Humanity" like that ChillingWorth losing his will for revenge, dies shortly and leaving Pearl a share of his property in England. This shows his humanity. After several years Hester returns to her cottage and resumes wearing scarlet letter. When she dies and buried near the grave of Dimmesdale. Their shared tomb had a single letter in black (A). Charles Dickens says, "A Loving Heart Is the Truest Wisdom." Here they are only expecting love not for money and stuff. Here the author has portrayed puritan's characterization. He has effectively sketched the character of a woman and her life struggles.

Reference

Hawthorne, Nathaniel. *The Scarlet Letter*. New York: Signet Classic, 1988.

Susan, Ketcham. Retrieved from the Digital Public Library of America

<https://dp.la/primary-source-sets/the-scarlet-letter-by-nathaniel-hawthorne>

CHAPTER FOURTEEN

SUPPRESSED VOLCANO IN SHASHI DESHPANDE'S "THAT LONG SILENCE"

R. Madubala,
II MA English,
Edayathangudy G. S. Pillay Arts & Science College (Autonomous),
Nagapattinam.

Since ancient times, women have faced many difficulties in exploring their identity, individual emotions, and feelings. Most of the novels by Deshpande portray women's struggles. *That long silence* starts with the role of an affectionate mother, dutiful to her in-laws and her relatives. The author expresses that a husband has not given attention to his wife's emotions, likes, and dislikes. The novel ends with the breaking of her long silence. From a very early stage, women have been under one control or another of patriarchy. She is controlled by her father until she reaches adulthood, at which point she becomes dependent on her husband. In ancient days, child marriage was in practice. The child faced a lot of issues in her life, both psychologically and physically. Everything happened to her when she was not even aware of what life was and it also ended in the same state. The 'Sati'system was in practise in the earlier centuries in India. After the abolition of 'Sati,' **the** status of women was recognized. Gradually, women started to attain education and many became writers. Through their writings, they created awareness of the empowerment of women.

Shashi Deshapande's *That Long Silence*reveals the struggles of a middle-class Indian woman. She has portrayed her female protagonist in a realistic manner. Suppression of women by men in society as revealed in *That Long Silence.* The male ego has given women an inferior status through the ages. Man has neglected her as a second-class citizen. Empower female writers like Shashi Deshpande, Arundhati Roy, and Anita Desai who have tried with sincerity and honesty to deal with the physical, psychological, and emotional stress syndrome of women in family and society.

In *That Long Silence*, the protagonist Jaya, from her younger days, though well educated, suffers a lot of frustrations. Her emotions and desire to hear the radio broadcast were blocked. She was treated as an unpaid servant for societal status after her marriage with Mohan. Due to rapid technological and scientific advancements, women are placed in various fields. But due to lack of communication between the family members, there is a misunderstanding. In most Indian cultural families, women are forced to tackle their family situation by offering their personal wealth. In this circumstance, women are mentally and physically affected and even forced to death.

In this novel, the protagonist is identified by two names. Jaya is the name of victory given by her father. Suhasini is the name given by her husband, who means soft, smiling, placid, and motherly. The change of name after marriage was customary in Maharastra. This reveals that nothing is permanent for women in society.

Protagonist Jaya gets married at the age of fifteen. She was driven by a strong desire to live her life solely for the happiness and fulfilment of her husband and two children. Her feelings and desires were not respected by her husband and family members. Due to Mohan's business loss, they shifted their family to 'Dadar Flat', where Jaya felt discomfort in all manners.

Days passed, her suppressed desire and emotions evoked to publish a novel. On reading the script, Mohan felt that his own life story was reflected. He gets separated from Jaya. Jaya, as a victorious woman, realises that communication gaps are the root cause of a successful and pleasant life.

Generally, in society, the feminine gender faces two roles in life. While the child is with her parents, she gets all sorts of comforts. But after marriage, she has to struggle a lot to fulfill her small desires. She is forced to work for the whole family. She dedicates her life to uplift and betterment of her children and other family members.

In this novel, Jaya, the protagonist, has to work to fulfil the desires of her husband Mohan and her two children. Jaya wanted to become a writer. She could not express her desire among the family members. Due to the lack of freedom of speech, her desires and emotions were suppressed. Finally, in the novel, she writes and publishes a story for the sake of money.

Her husband, on reading the story, hurts Jaya, saying that the story reveals his personal life and gets separated from her, and nobody in the family respected her feelings. There was no space for freedom of speech, which is the root cause of emotional depression.

In the olden days, women's children were not given education; she was indulged in doing all household activities. In the present era, though women have gotten well educated and placed in various fields, under family circumstances they are not given the opportunity to speak, share their ideas and emotions. Many women are adversely affected by this situation. They are mentally and physically affected a lot. That can be observed through "magazines and newspapers"in day-to-day life. Jaya is a female protagonist in *That Long Silence* who is considered a volcano and has the potential to express her thoughts and feelings like the burst of a volcano but is suppressed by the patriarchy.

Though Jaya was suppressed within the family circle, she has overcome the situation and published a novel, but her husband Mohan turns against this scenario and gets estranged from Jaya, which hurts Jaya a lot. She becomes speechless in this circumstance.

In this novel, Jaya's feelings are not given importance, and disrespect, disregard, and neglect of one's feelings and thoughts lead to psychological disorder and mental illness, which lead to death. In spite of vast scientific advancements in society, women are considered slaves in family circumstances. She is not given freedom of speech, freedom of thought, and freedom of equality even in society. Only when equality prevails among men and women can expect to see a better social environment.

Reference

Deshpande, Shashi. *That Long Silence*. Delhi: Penguin, 1989. Print.

CHAPTER FIFTEEN

OPPRESSION OF WOMEN IN GIRISH KARNAD'S "NAGAMANDALA"

Misma. S,
II MA English,
Infant Jesus College of Arts and Science for Women,
Mulagumoodu.

This paper depicts the oppression of women in the play *Nagamandala* by Girish Karnad. He is one of India's foremost playwrights, actors, and filmmakers. In *Naga-Mandala*, Karnad weaves two Kannada folk tales together. The first one comments on the paradoxical nature of oral tales in general: they have an existence of their own, independent of the teller, and yet they live only when they are passed on from one story-teller to another. Ensconced within this is the story of Rani, who makes up tales to fill the void in her life. Rani's predicament poignantly reflects the human need to live by fiction and half-truths.

Oppression is the inequitable use of authority, law, or physical force to prevent others from being free or equal. Oppression is a type of injustice. In some psychological views, the oppression of women is an outcome of the more aggressive and competitive nature of males due to testosterone levels. Others attribute it to a self-reinforcing cycle where men compete for power and control.

The protagonist of this play is Rani, which means queen. Rani's life after her marriage illustrates the life of every oppressed woman in our country. She is the only daughter of her parents. Her parents didn't give her an opportunity to choose her life partner. Her father found a suitable match for Rani, whose name was Appanna. The day she matured, she left with her husband. Her mother was crying, but she couldn't do anything. It shows that women have no power in their decisions. After their marriage, Appanna takes Rani to his house, which was far away from Rani's hometown. She had no one to talk to, so she talked to herself. Rani was imprisoned in the house and spent her days cooking and talking to herself. Once the housework was over, she had nothing to do. Whenever she tries to tell her husband that she is frightened of being alone at night, he is not willing to listen to her.

Rani looks at him nonplussed. He pays no attention to her, goes out, shuts the door, locks it from the outside, and goes away. She runs to the door, pushes it, finds it locked and peers out of the barred window. The below lines from the text clearly show her oppressed condition. "He is gone...She does not know what is happening and is perplexed. She cannot even weep. She goes and sits in a corner of her room. Talks to herself indistinctly" (18).

Karnad has illustrated domestic violence in this play. Appanna is a metaphor for Male Chauvinism presented in the drama Naga-Mandala. Appanna literally means "any man" and represents the metaphor of man in general, his chauvinistic stance and towering dominance to the extent of suppressing a woman's individuality. Appanna used to mistreat Rani throughout the play. When he found Rani was not in the kitchen, he slapped her and asked where she had been.

- APPANNA. Rani, where have you been?
- I said, where have you been? Rani, answer me!

- Rani moves aside so that she can go in. But the moment she steps in, Appanna slaps her hard. Rani collapses to the floor. He does not look at her again. Just pulls the door shut, locks it from outside, and goes away. There is not a trace of anger in anything he does. Just cold contempt. The dog barks loudly at the King Cobra which watches from behind the tree, hissing, excited and restless. Appanna goes away. Rani goes to her bedroom. Throws herself down in her usual corner, crying. (31)

He also beats her when he finds out that she is pregnant. He pushed her on the floor, kicked her, and queried her chastity. “RANI. Why are you humiliating me like this? Why are you stripping me naked in front of the whole village? Why don’t you kill me instead? I would have killed myself. But there’s not even a rope in this house for me to use” (49).

In the play, Karnad has portrayed two different kinds of women. Rani is submissive and afraid of her husband. On the other hand, Kurudavva is a courageous woman. Even though she is blind, she is the one who takes care of her son. She carried him everywhere. Unlike Rani, Kurdavva chose her husband. She shows her dominance even when they name their son. When Kappanna was born, her husband told her he was so fair, but Kurudavva was the one who suggested naming him Kappanna, which means ‘dark’. When she finds that Appanna has locked Rani in the house, she wants to help Rani. Her son, Kappanna advised her not to meddle in others’ lives. Even though he knows Appanna is rude to Rani, he doesn’t want to help her. “KAPPANNA. Mother, you can’t do this! You can’t start meddling in other people’s affairs the first thing in the morning. That Appanna should have been born a wild beast or a reptile. By some mistake, he got human birth. He can’t stand other people. Why do you want to tangle with him?” (19).

They both went to Appanna’s house just to check whether Rani was still there or if Appanna had sent her back to her parents' house. They were shocked because Appanna locked Rani at home. Kurudavva described Rani as a cage bird. However, when Kappanna is afraid to talk to Rani, Kurudavva is the one who talks to Rani and finds out that he comes home only once for lunch. She orders her son to bring the wooden box, which contains two pieces of roots. She advised Rani to make a paste and mix it with food.

Karnad also represents the unconditional love of Rani for her husband. Though Rani is mistreated by her husband, she has a devotion to him. When she made a paste of the root and mixed it in the milk, as soon as Appanna drank, he fell down. Rani was shocked to see this and wept for him when he was unconscious. Kurudavva says because of his concubine's spell, that small piece of root doesn't work on him. So she asked her to use the large piece. Rani is concerned about her husband's health. As soon as she made the paste, it turned into blood.

- Suppose something happens to my husband? What will my fate be? That little piece made him ill. Who knows ... ?

(Slaps herself on her cheeks.)

- No, no. Forgive me, God. This is evil. I was about to commit a crime. Father, Mother, how could I, your daughter, agree to such a heinous act? No, I must get rid of this before he notices anything. (30)

However, at the end, the play represents women's empowerment. The snake ordeal, which Rani undergoes to prove her marital purity, provides the irony of the situation. Appanna accused her of being a 'whore'. The typical discriminating treatment of Appanna and Rani is carefully presented in the play. Nobody is against it. Even the village elders who sit in judgement of Rani's adultery do not find any fault with him. Nobody believes the innocence of Rani. She sleeps with Naga without knowing her identity. She does not discover the identity of Naga, who assumes Appanna's form by using its magical power. They all go to the ant hill, where Rani bows down and picks up a snake, declaring that if she is pure, the snake would not harm her. This snake happens to be the very snake that impregnated Rani. Thus, Rani escapes unhurt and the village adores her.

- ELDER 1. Appanna, your wife is not an ordinary woman. She (ELDER is a goddess incarnate. Don't grieve that you judged her wrongly and treated her badly. That is how goddesses reveal themselves to the world. You were the chosen instrument for the revelation of her divinity.
- ELDER 2. Spend the rest of your life in her service. You need merit in ten past lives to be chosen for such holy duty. (57)

In this play, Karnad cleverly depicts the state of a representative Indian woman, controlled by the patriarchal order and constrained by convention, but whose temperament is uninhibited. This play can be studied from the feministic point of view, which is an important discussion in today's society. The playwright has successfully presented female subjugation at the hands of patriarchal power, which is a contemporary social reality.

Reference

Karnad, Girish. *Three Plays: Naga-Mandala, Hayavadana, Tughlaq.* New Delhi: Oxford India Paperback, 1999.

https://en.m.wikipedia.org/wiki/Nagamandala

https://www.thoughtco.com/oppression-womens-history-definiti

Dhanavel, P. *The Indian Imagination of Girish Karnad: Essays on Hayavadana*, India: Prestige Books, 2000.Dodiya, Jaydipsinh.

CHAPTER SIXTEEN

Racial Discrimination in Paul Beatty's "The Sellout"

[1]**M. Monisha**, M.A. English (2019-2021),
[2]**Dr. N. Asharudeen**, Assistant Professor of English,
Edayathangudy G. S. Pillay Arts and Science College
(Autonomous),
Nagapattinam.

The unnamed narrator of the novel is a protagonist who lives in Dickens, on the outskirts of Los Angeles. The backdrop of the entire novel is set in the ghetto community. He was brought up in the circumstances of racial discrimination. His father is a sociologist who raises his voice against racism wherever it depresses black people. As a social protestant, he has responsibilities to look after the oppressed society, and the effect of his responsibilities, as well as the existence of racial discrimination in society, creates barriers to his son's education at a white public school. He does some social experiments through his son to convince him that racism really exists around him.

Beatty has depicted a strange situation in which the protagonist, the unnamed narrator of the novel, faces racial discrimination at a gas station. The gas station is run by a White where the protagonist seeks permission to use the restroom, but he is instructed to buy a coke by paying the amount of $1.50. The cost of the coke fixed for Black is higher than that for White. The actual price of the coke is seven cents only. This drastic incident affects the protagonist and convinces him to believe racial discrimination strongly exists in his society. The depressive state of mind against racism started only after the death of his father; he was shot dead by police.

After the death of his father, he tries to own his father's belongings in different ways. But, he is criticised as the "nigger whisperer" by the people of Dickens when he attempts to acquire the property. Then he is stunned by the exclusion of his home land from the map, which induces him to worry about the value of the land. So, he decides to recover his homeland. For the sake of recovering the land, he discusses it with the well-known group of his late father. At that time, there is a person called Little Rascal whose actual name is Hominy Jenkins, who has also suffered a lot by losing his home town. After he comes to know the drastic situation of the protagonist, he decides to help him to bring back Dickens at any cost.

The author has meticulously depicted the divisions of two races that can be clearly observed in his portrayal of the segregated city bus, where the stickers are affixed and labelled 'one third of seats reserved for the white people'. Then he starts his work of bringing awareness about discrimination at Chaff Middle School. Charisma helps him to segregate at the school and makes them believe completely in the development of black kids' education. Meanwhile, the narrator and Hominy Jenkins paint the borders, making a mark of segregation. After that, the narrator tries to unite the white students at Chaff Middle School, but Charisma stops the students from entering the school. This occurrence reveals the confused state of the narrator as well as the instability of society because he is accused of segregating students in the city and encouraging slavery.

Then he is taken to the court for this case, and he is unaware of whether he goes to prison or not, but he is pleased that his home land is enlisted on the map again. Hominy Jenkins also decides to get away from him.

The entire novel deals with the crisis of racism in the contemporary society of the United States of America. Beatty portrays the abolishment of black majority cities like Dickens. Despite the end of slavery in 1964, black people are still oppressed in the twenty-first century. Paul Beatty wished to depict actual circumstances of suppressed society that can be clearly observed in *The Sellout*.

Reference

Beatty, Paul. *The Sellout*. Picador Books, 2015.

CHAPTER SEVENTEEN

"A Christmas Carol": A Study

Ragavi. G (2020-2022),
MA English,
Edayathangudy G. S. Pillay Arts & Science College
(Autonomous),
Nagapattinam.

A Christmas Carol is one of Charles Dickens' most well-known novels, and it is full of incredible parallels and motifs that pervade it and fill it with great beauty.The redemption of Scrooge and the comparison with Tiny Tim is one of the most moving moments in literature focusing primarily on the power of conviction. The progression of Scrooge from tight fisted miser to generous philanthropist is one of the most moving episodes in literature.

In the beginning, Scrooge is a hard hearted and cruel character who is completely possessed by money. He does not even want to grant his faithful and ill-used clerk Bob Cratchit a day off on Christmas Day and bawls about Christmas being a "humbug'. On the contrary, Bob Cratchit is happy with his lot even though he is desperately poor and without any hope of improving his situation under the iron rule of his master, Scrooge.

One cannot say that Scrooge was happy even when he encountered those who were attempting to make life easier for the poor. He dismisses them by telling them that he wants to be put down for nothing and that they should leave him to celebrate Christmas in his own way. It appears that he is not too popular amongst his peers and elders, even in the opening description. The novel's themes are redemption and remorse, which are experienced on several levels by Scrooge as he is made to recall his past, assess his present, and contemplate his future. His late partner, Jacob Marley, was also a terribly tight-fisted man, and when he visited him in the dead of night, Scrooge attempted to make merry and joke with him, but the heavy-paced ghost was having none of this and began stamping around in a rage.

Scrooge is an old miser, and the views of Christmas past bring back terrible memories for him. He reviews his childhood, where he ended up alone in class with his dear sister coming for him and taking him home. This appears to be one of the main sorrowful points in his life, as is the situation when his girlfriend leaves him, as he has become too atavistic and materialist.

Scrooge is very happy when he works under Fezziwig, who is a kind and gentle friend apart from being his master. Here one can view the complete contrast with the way Scrooge treats his clerk, Bob Cratchit, who is kept "in a sort of tank" while he freezes without having any heating in the office and writes away furiously. In fact, remorse immediately strikes Scrooge when he views the spirits attempting to intervene, but 'they have lost this power for ever'.

On the contrary, Bob Cratchit attempts to make merry out of every situation, even though he is poor. The charity embodied by the two people cannot be more different. Scrooge is a hard-fisted, mean old miser, while Cratchit is a penniless clerk with a large brood of children to his name. Despite the fact that the Cratchits are almost penniless, they find joy in almost everything, including the way they prepare for the Christmas festivities.And then there is Tiny Tim, the frail child who is a cripple but is also cheerful and observant of the world, especially when he quotes the scriptures and observes that Jesus made blind men see and lame beggars walk.

In a sense, the Cratchit family is a mirror image of the family life that Dickens wanted for himself but could never achieve, even when he had wealth, fame, and fortune. The fact that he was sent to a blacking factory at the early age of twelve rankled inside him for a long time, and the avid description of Cratchit's working conditions is perhaps a mirror image of this life.

The description offered by the Ghost of Christmas Present also demonstrates that Scrooge is actually a good-hearted man since he begins to see himself for what he really is. His observance of his nephew Fred as he celebrates Christmas with his friends continues to affect him deeply, and he desperately wishes to join in the happiness of the festivities. The dark cloud of death hangs over Scrooge once again when the spirit tells him, 'I see an empty chair at the table and a crutch without an owner in the corner"—a bleak yet direct reference to Tiny Tim's impending demise. However, the most powerful scene is at the end of the spirit's visit when he shows him two children, a boy called Ignorance and a girl called Want. When Scrooge asks if they had any refuge or resource, the spirit answers coldly with Scrooge's own words, "Are there no prisons? Are there no workhouses?", making the money lender hang his head in shame and remorse. Here, one begins to sense that Scrooge is slowly transforming himself.

The visit of the third and final spirit is perhaps the one which is the most eye-opening of the three. This spirit does not talk but merely points in different directions. The description of Scrooge's death is very realistic, and one can observe the depths to which he had descended when the charity lady and undertaker fight over themselves to sell his possessions. Scrooge realises that his life is not worth living in its current state and has already begun making plans to change. Another powerful scene shows the joy imbued in that young couple who were about to be thrown out of their abode when the man discovers that Scrooge is dead and will not leave them homeless after all. And finally, when Scrooge falls into his own grave, he wakes up to find that the grave was a lamppost and it was all just a dream.

The comparisons between Scrooge and the Cratchit family are a consistent leitmotif of the novel, which culminates in joy and happiness as Scrooge becomes a generous and heartful man. The transformation is one of the most beautiful moments in literature, especially when he goes to his nephew Fred and asks if he would have him, with Fred cheerfully and heartily stating that of course he would. Here one can observe that Scrooge's moral character is good indeed, for although he was completely overwhelmed by avarice and money, he definitely changed and became a far better person overnight. This meant that, in his heart of hearts, he was certainly not a bad person at all but was just enveloped in misery and self-thought. His preoccupation with money vanished overnight, and he definitely heeded Marley's warning.

However, the transformation is complete when Scrooge feigns being angry at Bob Cratchit after the latter has made merry on Christmas day. Scrooge could not keep up with his acting and burst out in joy and generosity.

The masterpiece that is *A Christmas Carol* is reflected in the manner in which Dickens skillfully conveys a scene where happiness and remorse are intermingled with each other. Scrooge is finally free when he manages to unshackle himself from the chains of selfishness and avarice and finds true happiness when he is with others, as well as being a father to Tiny Tim. It is perhaps the greatest story of Christmas and is so replete with wonderful messages and events that we seem to be in a trance when reading it. The element of progression is there all the time for us to see, and we can only feel that life has a meaning, which is conveyed through Christmas.

Reference

Dickens, Charles. *A Christmas Carol and Other Stories.* New York: Modern Library, 1995.

CHAPTER EIGHTEEN

"THIRTEEN REASONS WHY": AN EPISTOLARY NOVEL

[1]**M.Sailaxmi,** MA English, (2019-2021),
[2]**P. Muthukumar**, Assistant Professor of English,
Edayathangudy G. S. Pillay Arts & Science College
(Autonomous),
Nagapattinam.

This study attempts to focus on an epistolary novel, a sequel to written records. Usually, sequel records are available as letters, diaries, and sequel plots in newspapers. This sort of written record possesses a real story or a story depicted in a realistic setup. It can also express different points of view without an alternative choice to the device of an omniscient narrator. *Thirteen Reasons Why* is a novel by Jay Asher in which he uses the source of modern electronic devices, recording stereotypic tapes in this work. The author of the novel has focused on the death of a girl named Hannah, who committed suicide, a real life incident. Before her death, she left recorded voices in stereotypes as evidence in which she expressed the reasons behind her terrible decision. She made a plan to circulate the recorded stereotype voices. Jay Asher has used the tapes to deliver Hannah's voice so lively. When her voice entered the public platform, people had to hear her voice in a sequential manner that made them feel heavy. But the voice had already started to circulate two weeks before her death, when she was alive. People wanted to hear her voice because they wanted to see how she revealed some names behind her bad decision again."Hello, boys and girls. Hannah Baker here. Live and in stereo... No return engagements. No encore. And this time, absolutely no Requests" (7).

When Hannah Baker starts to speak, she tells that 'live in stereo' even after she died. She wanted to live through her voice in stereo and also wanted to tell her people what their mistakes were. What made her take this decision? She wanted to create an impact among them. It is not ordinary tapes to just pass on by them, but tapes by a poor girl who couldn't make it through. A small thing done by Alex for fun made a list of "who's hot who's not" and destroyed Hannah's reputation. She was treated by others to take her for granted. He never knew that he would come across this tape until he heard it. Why Hannah chose tapes even though she has a mobile phone and is also an active person on social media is because she avoided the provisions of social media to keep her privacy. She wasn't able to stop rumours about her when she was alive. People always show interest in her life only to spread rumours about her. They even made stories about her. Her classmates were curious to spread rumours in Hannah's life rather than help her. "And she was so new to school that the rumors overshadowed everything else I knew about her" (30).

Hannah used the stereo voice records to reveal her life so vividly, but in some spaces in her voice she pauses, probably because she is afraid of revealing the names of people who actually disturbed her because they are the reason behind her terrible decision, death. Clay, the protagonist of the novel, is frightened when he begins to hear Hannah's because she says, "I I hope you're ready, because I'm about to tell you the story of my life. More specifically, why my life ended. And if you're listening to these tapess, You're one of the reasons why" (7).

It insists that her acquaintances are the reasons for her decision; he becomes anxious about his mistake. But he slowly follows the voice of the stereo tape, which was created by Hannah to connect the events in which she described her problems. Clay wants to wander the places which she depicted in tapes to feel Hannah's voice. That gives a lively feel to this novel. Hannah also peeled off some tiger under cow skin like Zach. Before Hannah opens up about him, Clay believes Zach was a good guy, but he is not. He doesn't want anybody to gossip about him even though he was the reason for those mistakes. He steals a note from Hannah's notes of encouragement and pretends that she never gets notes from anyone. Zach created this to make people believe that she was avoided by everyone. When Hannah said about those notes, "I needed those notes. I needed any hope those notes might have offered" (165).

After hearing this, Clay wants to know more about Hannah. Even though he was with her when she was alive, he never knew that she had gone through much suffering in her life. Hannah's voice reveals the pain she suffered a lot, and her words in the stereotypical tapes express her pain. She was longing for a simple note to revive her with hope. Not all the names mentioned in the tapes were mistaken. Clay Jensen is always nice to Hannah. Clay even reacts to the people who treat Hannah poorly. But Clay comes to know everything only through tapes. It means that if he knew everything about her decision, he would definitely try his best to stop her. She reveals everything in the tape, including her private life. But she failed to reveal it to Clay. If it happened, she would be alive. He could have definitely given her a reason to live. The names of the twelve members come out through Hannah's voice. She reveals what they did to her, but they cannot change the past. They can only feel the pain and realise their mistakes. "You can't stop the future. You can't rewind the past. The only way to learn the secret ... is to press play" (Back of the book).

It is revealed even in her voice itself. The deeds of every person possibly have an impact on others' lives. The life of Hannah is definitely a great lesson for everyone; it makes people understand the value of words that are regularly used in human life.

Reference:

Asher, Jay. *13 Reasons Why*. New Delhi: Penguin Random House UK, 2009. Print.

CHAPTER NINETEEN

A Comparative Study on "The Spanish Tragedy" and "The Fire and the Rain"

M. Shanmathi,
Assistant Professor of English,
Rabiammal Ahamed Maideen College for Women,
Thiruvarur.

Lorenzo, brother of Belimperia in *The Spanish Tragedy*. He is a vile man who steals a glory of his fellow soldiers. He treats his sister badly and locked her in the room. He is a man without a heart. He is ready to do anything for his achievement. Lorenzo is a Machiavellian villain who utilizes Pedringano and serberine for all his crimes but betrays them and kill them. He is the one who poisons Balthazar's mind in the name of his love. Lorenzo is the one of the murderers along with Balthazar and murdered Horatio. In The *Fire and The Rain*, Parvasu is a crooked man in both thoughts and actions. He is unemotional and rational. He kills his own father Raibhya, out of hatredness on him. A villain by nature

Parvasu treacherously bears the blame of patricide on his young brother Arvasu. Parvasu is a heartless person. Brother characters are portrayed as villain in these plays.

Hieronimo, protagonist of *The Spanish Tragedy* is terribly upset due to his son Horatio's murder. He cries out of pain and depression, plans to commit suicide then rejects for the sake of taking revenge for his son's murderers. He meets the king and demanding for justice but he was neglected by the King of Spain. In *the Fire and The Rain*, Arvasu owns the responsibility for Raibhya's murder and Parvasu makes him a victim for the crimes that he gets committed. He orders the Brahmins to throw Arvasu out of the sanctified precincts. Protagonists of the plays are suffered a lot by the death of their blood relatives.

The death of Don Andrea in the Battle field is the reason that Belimperia requests Horatio to be her lover in order to take revenge for Andrea's death. Belimperia's love for Horatio is the reason of his death. It makes Hieronimo become furious and decide to take avenge on the murderers of his son. The love affair between Yavakri and Vishakha is the reason for death of Raibhya and Yavakri in *The Fire and the Rain*. The blame of Raibhya's death falls on Arvasu . It leads him to take avenge on Parvasu. The significant changes arise only after the death of beloved characters in these plays.

In *The Spanish Tragedy*, Andrea is betrayed by Balthazar. Andrea fights bravely in the battlefield but Balthazar fails to appreciate him. Balthazar feels jealous of him and kills him cunningly. Lorenzo uses Pedringano and Serberine for all his crimes but betrays them and kills them at the end of the play. In *The Fire and The Rain*, Parvasu uses Arvasu and betrays him and cunningly blames for the death of Raibhya.

Initially, Belimperia loves Andrea but after his death she falls in love with Horatio. In *The Fire and The Rain*, Vishakha loves Yavakri initially and in the absence of him for ten years. She is married to Parvasu and also loves him.

Both the plays revolve around supernatural elements. The Ghost of Andrea in *Spanish Tragedy* and spirit of revenge informs the audience about his death and he wants to take revenge upon his murderers. The ghost arrives at the underworld due to his unperformed funeral rites. Then queen Prosperine, the wife of the King of underworld Pluto offers him to revenge on his murderers. Throughout the play, the ghost of Andrea travels along with the other characters. In *The Fire and The Rain,* Brahma Rakshasa is raised by Raibhya to kill Yavakri for the love affair between his daughter-in-law Vishakha and Yavakri.

The Ghost of Andrea and Brahma Rakshasha wants salvation. The ghost of Andrea arrives at hell due to his unperformed funeral rites. Then Andrea along with the spirit of revenge to take revenge against the murderers and ghost of Andreea gets salvation only at the end of the play. Brahma Rakshasha wants salvation. He informs Parvasu that when he was alive, he was bad. After his death he is no longer reborn as an ordinary mortal human. He becomes a Brahma Rakshasha "a soul locked in nothingness". He feels that it is an unimaginably horrible existence. He requests Parvasu to liberate him. He wants to fade away like nothing. But Parvasu denies. In the end of the play, Brahma Rakshasha gets salvation by Arvasu's wish from God Indra.

Both the plays have the techniques of 'play within a play'. *Soliman and Perseda* is staged in *The Spanish Tragedy*. It was written by Hieronimo, The protoganist of the play who plays a role of Bashaw. The role of Perseda is played by Belimperia. Perseda falls in love with a knighty named Erastus, played by Lorenzo. They get married. But Turkish Emperor Soliman is played by Balthazar falls in love with Perseda and kills Erastus by the idea of his noble courtier Bashaw. Perseda becomes furious for the death of her husband. She in turns kills Soliman and stabs herself to death. All the characters are really killed themselves in the play. Then Hieronimo reveals the truth that all his plan to revenge his son's death. In *The Fire and The Rain,* ' The Triumph of Lord Indra', is staged. The role of Vritra is played by Arvasu. The role of Indra is played by actor manager and the Vishwarupa is played by another actor. Indra proclaims himself as the king of gods and the son of

Brahmaa, the father of all creations. He treats inferior for the mortal son who was born by Brahmaa on the human womb. So he wants to destroy Vishwarupa who is the mortal son. Indra informs that he is conducting fire sacrifice in their father's memory. He invites Vishwarupa and killed him. Vritra is a demon born by Indra aware him by Indra's plan but Vishwarupa trust Indra and dies. This play makes Parvasu guilty and reveals the truth behind Raibhya's death to the audience. Both the protagonist takes revenge their villains by the play are enacted in the stage.

In these plays, lady love of the protagonist is died. Hieronimo's wife Isabella, goes mad and stabs herself to death at the place where Horatio was hanged to overcome his grief towards his son's death. In *The Fire and The Rain*, Nittilai the lady love of the protagonist arvasu was killed by her husband with a knife and throws her on the ground. In the end of the play, both the desire of the protagonists is fulfilled. They stand for justice, and the common theme of love, revenge, salvation, supernaturalism and death are the similarities exist in *The Spanish Tragedy* and *The Fire and the Rain*.

Reference

Karnad, Girish. *The Fire and the Rain*. India: Oxford U P, 1998. Print

Kyd, Thomas, Andrew Gurr, and J R. Mulryne. *The Spanish Tragedy*. London: Methuen

Drama, 2009. Print.

CHAPTER TWENTY

OPPRESSION DUE TO CASTE SYSTEM AND SUPERIORITY IN ADIGA'S "THE WHITE TIGER"

Shimna.S,
II M A English,
Infant Jesus College of Arts and Science for Women,
Mulagumoodu.

India is a diverse nation with individuals of various castes and religions . Indian English in writing is adopted by writers throughout India by nationality and they belong to different regions with spoken and written knowledge of their own different dialects and local language. Their writings always display the regional themes based on their origin and background.

The White Tiger portrays the issues related with social domination based on the life of Balram. Low wages with long working hours is a usual happening for low caste domestic workers in India. Adiga exposed the real state of the dim and light India. The class of the individuals alone is considered by the employers. Such working class members of the society are too fragile, deprived, and powerless to oppose their Employer's exploitment.

Balram was an exception to the system in this scenario governed by Indian culture. Investigation reveals that these individuals cannot look for escape based on law and ethic. In the novel Adiga illustrates how the rich individual, the law enforcer and the lawmaker is using this system to take the best advantages with these socially deprived and denied individuals. *The White Tiger* depicts these issues through Balram's story. Adiga displays the voice and emotions of India's underclass. India's culture is filled with cruel traditions and merciless practices through class and caste discrimination and thus denied the changes over proficient individuals.

In *The White Tiger,* the deprived inhabitants of Laxmangarh chose to move to the city for better advancement in life. This reflects that migration is a typical story for such small towns in rural India. The essential need for a satisfied and comfortable existence of life is denied in such parts of places in India. The pitiable living conditions of these areas are reflected through lack of finances, joblessness and lack of opportunity. It finally drives a notable number of population to seek refuge in urban areas of India. Such a compelling circumstance occurs in the life of Balram to seek his fortune in urban India.

The White Tiger explores poverty, injustice, adversities, anxieties, and oppressed delivers a dark side of India's class struggle through the narration of Balram Halwai, a village boy. Adiga says his novel attempts to hear the voice of the every man live in each and every corner through India.

According to Adiga most of the poor people hail from Bihar, Bangladesh and Nepal. They get low paid jobs by working like drivers, domestic help, cook, construction workers, and gardeners and as a side they have to take care of all the needs of their masters. Adiga's novel emphases the difficulties faced by poor people who are living under severe poverty condition. It attacks the economic disparities, class struggle, injustice, poverty, and inequalities. It is the story of a poor rickshaw wallah who moves from the darkness of the rural India to the light of urban Gurgaon. In this novel, Aravind Adiga tells the terrible story of a young man who cruelly murder's his employer and gets away with his money.

The narrative is centred on two characters, Balram and Ashok. Balram was born to a poverty originates from a little town but his master Ashok is well settled with good financial set up, politically well connected because of his family's background. Balram was naturally affected by what he saw happening around him. Ashok makes Balram to get acquainted with his deals and allow him to handle crores of rupees on his own behalf and thus introduced him to the big time corruption and power broking. In this novel, Adiga portrays how the lower caste people suffered and they were alsooppressed by the landlords and upper caste people. The lower caste people have to struggle hard for their day today life. They were highly exploited by the landlords. Balram also suffered under the landlords. Through the character of the landlords, Adiga deals with the theme of Casteism that prevails in Indian society. Being born in such a low caste would result in a differed treatment as servants; not just like in an upper caste family, they a human being.

The novel shows the real faces of Indian society. Balram's journey from Laxmangarh to Dhanbad, Dhanbad difference between the life of to Delhi, Delhi to Bangalore, tells us the rural and urban, rich and poor society. In the beginning of the novel, the novelists present the rural poverty and the deplorable condition health and education system of India. It is due to extreme poverty that creates darkness in the life of the rural as well as urban society and thus it perpetuates the sufferings of the lower class Lower class has no place in such caste dominated society.They are always deprived from their rights and they have to suffer and remain silent. When Balram went to Strok's home at first Stork asked him,

"Are you from a top caste or bottom caste, boy?" (64). So, Balram replied him, Bottom. Then Stork's son Mukesh and Stork started talking about their servant's caste. "All our employees are top caste. It won't hurt to have one or two bottom castes working for us" (65).

Balram belonged to the lower class and whenever and wherever he search for a job, he suffered a lot and all questioned about his caste. Stork's employees belonged to the upper caste; one or two are from lower caste.

Adiga highlights the relationship between the masters and servants. The masters never thought about their servants and their family. They were always survived with money-making motive and hence they lacked humanitarian attitude. Throughout the story of Balram, he suffered a lot due to being born in a lower caste family. Dueto his family situation he discontinued his education and went to the job. Balrama wanted to become a successful Entrepreneur. At the end of the story as he wished Balram become a successful Entrepreneur. As Balram belonged to a lower caste and since he was in a state of poverty stricken, his master treated him cruelly. This brought a change in the mind of Balram to go to extreme level of murdering his master and thus he becomes an Entrepreneur.

Balram Halwai, is presented as a modern Indian hero, from the economic prosperity of India in the recent past. Balram wants to escape from the Rooster Coop. Having been a witness to all of Ashok's corrupt practices and gambling with money to buy politicians, to kill and to loot, he decides to steal and kill. Adiga delves deep into his subconscious as he plans to loot Rs.700,000 stuffed into the red bag.

His climbing over the ladder of success is by murdering Mr. Ashok, his employer, and stealing his bag full of money – Rs.700,000/. All this happened only based on a philosophy of revenge, ambition and corruption.

His thirst for freedom came alive when he visited his native village while Mr. Ashok and wife Pinky went on an excursion. It can be evident through this below quoted lines

- ...I swam through the pond, walked up the hill...and entered the Black Fort for the first time...Putting my foot on the wall, I looked down on the village from there. My little Laxmangarh. I

> saw the temple tower, the market, the glistening line of sewage, the landlords' mansion – and my own house, with that dark little cloud outside – the water buffalo. It looked like the most beautiful sight on earth. I leaned out from the edge of the fort in the direction of my village – and then I did something too disgusting to describe to you. Well actually, I spat. Again and again. And then, whistling and humming, I went back down the hill. Eight months later, I slit Mr Ashok's throat. (41-42)

The money is sufficient for him to begin a new life with a house of his own, a motorbike and a small shop. He implemented the murder plan in a quick intention: "The dream of the rich, and the dreams of the poor – they never overlap, do they? See, the poor dream all their lives of getting enough to eat and looking like the rich. And what do the rich dream of? Losing weight and looking like the poor" (225).

Adiga makes the protagonist spell out the way enterprising drivers make a little extra money.The novel has a well written social commentary on the poor rich divide in India. Thus the novel provides a dark pathetic perspective of India's class struggle in a globalized world through a retrospective narration from the protagonist. According to Adiga poor people are the victim of economic inequality of our society and this can be evident through the character of Balram Halwai in *The White Tiger.*

Reference

Adiga, Aravind. *The White Tiger*, New Delhi, Harper Collins.2008.

A conversation with AravindAdiga.*The White Tiger: A Novel.* New York: Print. Free,

2008: 284-288.

Agarwal, Beena. *Delhi as a Metaphor of Post-Industrial India in The White Tiger.*

Aravind Adiga's *The White Tiger: A Symposium of Critical Response*. Ed. R. K. Dhawan.

New Delhi: Prestige, 2011,pp 168- 173. Print.

Gurwara, Simmi. *AravindAdiga's White Tiger: A Study in Social Criticism*. The 11.

Vedic Path. 83.3 and 4 July. 2010.

Donahue, Deirdre. "Review." USA Today April, 2008.

http://www.usatoday.com/life/books/reviews/
2008-04-23-roundup-debutnovels_N.html

Sebastian. A.J. *Poor-Rich Divide in AravindAdiga's The White Tiger.* Journal of Alternative Perspectives in the Social Sciences (2009) Vol 1, No 2, 229-245.

Mahal, Ramandeep and Maharishi Markandeshwar. *An Analytical Study of Aravind*

Adiga's The White Tiger. International Journal of Psychosocial Rehabilitation, Vol. 24, Issue 06, 2020 .

Meenakshi .V. Journal of Xi'an Shiyou University, Natural Science Edition Vol. 17(03) 64-72

http://xisdxjxsu.asia *Castiesm in AravindAdiga's The White Tiger.*

CHAPTER TWENTY-ONE

Child Maltreated in Society Reflected in "Oliver Twist"

K. Siva Dharshni, (2020-2022),
MA English,
Edayathangudy G.S.Pillay Arts and Science College (Autonomous),
Nagapattinam.

Charles John Huffam Dickens, also known as Charles Dickens, who is the author of the novel *Oliver Twist,* was born on February 7, 1812 in Hampshire, England. He is an English writer and social critic, also regarded as the greatest novelist of the Victorian era. His notable works are *A Tale of Two Cities, Great Expectations, David Copperfield, A Christmas Carol, Nicholas Nickelby,* and *Oliver Twist*. Charles was also famous for hisnovels, short stories, comics, and novellas.

Dickens started to write his novel *Oliver Twist* under the Poor Lawof 1834, which halted government payments to the poor. And that's how *Oliver Twist* reflected on Social Criticism, which focuses on poverty in 19th century, London. *Oliver Twist,* Charles Dickens's second novel, was published as a three-volume book which portrays the sordid lives of criminals and expresses the sufferings of many orphans in London in the mid-19th century. This novel is a fiction and social novel.

Oliver Twist deals with the story of an orphan child living in London who fends for himself by joining a pickpocket's gang. This novel portrays Dickens' own childhood working in factories. In 1837, he began publishing the novel in instalments in his magazine, *Bentley's Miscellany*. Charles Dickens's main objectives in this novel were to raise awareness about the situations that the children had to face and live in to make money. The main theme of *Oliver Twist* describes how the poorest people in this society were maltreated. This is one of the key themes of *Oliver Twist,* where it represents the failure of the workhouse system, which is unable to take care of the poor and orphans. The important characters in this novel are Fagin, Oliver Twist, Nancy, Rose Maylie, Mr. Brownlow, Monks, Bill Sikes, Mr. and Mrs. Sowerberry, and some others who enacted their roles.

This research study reveals how children are maltreated by society. This novelfocuses on four kinds of child abuse: physical abuse, psychological abuse, sexual abuse,and social abuse. Let us look deep into this novel and describe some examples of these four kinds that express the sufferings of Oliver Twist. Physical abuse is an act which can cause damage to your physical body, like hitting, slapping, and threats with a weapon or even murder. Physical abuse is well known for the marks it leaves on a child's body, such as fractures, blood clots, and other hard damage. Oliver has experienced this physical abuse a lot when the master aimed a blow at Oliver's head with the ladle, restrained him in his arm, and screamed aloud for the beadle.

Psychological violence describes the behaviour that is intended to intimate and persecute, threaten or misuse authority, supervise, take the rights of the child, etc. Oliver has experienced this psychological abuse when Mr. Bumble threatened Oliver with a gentle hint, intimidated Oliver with a high voice, and ordered Oliver to mind what Mr. Bumble told him to.

Sexual abuse is one of the sexual intercourse practises by means of violence and values of religion, which include rape, incest, and exploitation. Oliver was sexually abused as a newborn, and the people around him predicted that he would end up in an orphanage and suffer, but no one pitied him.

In this context, social abuse represents neglect. Neglect is a behaviour that doesn't focus on the proper growth process of children. Oliver has experienced one of these forms of social abuse, which is neglect, when he was left alone in the coffin maker's shop. Throughout this study, we observed Dickens's objectives of parenting on children by society, nature, or substitute parents. He expresses many categories of child maltreatment. And this research study mainly focuses on physical abuse and neglect in social abuse. This must be more concerning to parents today for their children.

Dickens tries to reveal his lost childhood through the numerous child characters whom he made to live in this novel. Child abuse was linked to the latter's consequences. In the nineteenth century, the conflict between money and love eventually played a role in the welfare of children. He emphasised irresponsibility toward children in this novel. He exposes the readers to the pathetic conditions of the poor, especially the orphans and the children living below the poverty line in nineteenth century society. Charles Dickens delivers the social drawbacks in this novel, *Oliver Twist,* considered as the book of child maltreatment in the Victorian era. As the novel progresses, the drawbacks of the orphanage and the hidden world of nineteenth century society become apparent which exposes the child protagonist, Oliver,who experienced an extremely harsh life in a very hard situation until he found his benefactor.Right from the birth of Oliver Twist, he was under starvation, suppression, corruption, and violence.

Child maltreatment and neglect were discovered in the 1960's and 1970's. Instead, he honestly expresses his disapproval when there has been an acceptance of Victorian England. The ineffective poor law, child labour, and pathetic conditions of orphanages have been dealt with unsparing honesty. Dickens shows that the struggle of Oliver is not just about surviving but also about his desire to overcome the fear of being completely cut off from the outer world. The author of this novel, *Oliver Twist,*grabs the reader's attention and drags him into various **social evils** prevalent in contemporary society.

Dickens was the first great urban novelist in England and also one of the most important social commentators who used fiction effectively to criticise the economic, social, and moral abuses in the Victorian era. Child **maltreatment** is really bad treatment of children by their parents or other people who must actually take care of them. This study shows an individual pitted against society throughout the character of **Oliver**, who tries his best to come out of that hard-struggling situation and finally succeeds. Sufferings stand at the centre of the text. The novel at first opens with the troublesome life of Oliver's mother. Oliver's own life too shows the sufferings of others who become victims of poverty, the exploitative system and finally fall into the hands of criminal gangs. This research study aims to analyse this novel through the theory of psychoanalytic perspective.

This research study "Child Maltreated in Society Reflected in Oliver Twist" presents a horrible picture of child maltreatment in the society on which the future hinges. The institutionalization of this abuse is expressed in the uncaring doctor and the drunken nurse who attended Oliver's mother's delivery, and later, Oliver faces thrashing and hunger at the orphanage. This research represents the reality of how poor children were locked up in a dark place and faced emotional and physical abuse in the warehouse. His journey from an orphanage to an individual's freedom life helps this research study to declare how these inhumane practises were systematized.

Reference

Rogers, Richard, and Charles Dickens. *Oliver Twist.* Oxford: Oxford University Press, 2008. Print.

CHAPTER TWENTY-TWO

Gender Discrimination in Mahesh Dattani's "Tara"

M. Suganya,
II MA English,
Edayathangudy G. S. Pillay Arts & Science College
(Autonomous),
Nagapattinam.

Mahesh Dattani is one of the prominent playwrights on Indian Literature, who has written many plays such as *Final Solution*, *Dance Like a Man*, *Bravely Fought the Queen*, *On a Muggy Night in Mumbai*, *Tara*, *Thirty Days in September*, and *The Big Fat City*. He is the first playwright in English to be awarded the Sahitya Academy award. Dattani's two-act play *Tara*, tells the story of Chandan and Tara, who are conjoined twins and surgically separated in an unequal manner intended to favor the boy. *Tara* portrays the inequality of Indian society. Dattani has depicted the condition of women and gender discrimination, inequality, and patriarchy. *Tara* is a story about a girl born into an Indian family who faces many challenges. A girl born into an Indian family is exploited in some way.

The play *Tara* opens in London with Chandan, who has changed his name to Dan, a playwright trying to write a story. He recollects his past memories; the childhood days come to mind, the happy moments with Tara. When they were in the womb, they were together, and they were separated when they came out into the world. Dan writes his own story in his book. He begins the story by saying, “The Way we started in Life. Two lives and one body in one comfortable womb. Till we were forced out and separated” (CP 325). From the beginning of the play, Dattani portrayed gender discrimination, inequality, and patriarchy through the character of Patel, the father of Chandan and Tara. Patel concentrates only on Chandan because he is the male heir to their family. He was never concerned about Tara. Chandan’s father insists that he study well, and he has a plan for Chandan’s higher studies in London. He doesn’t even care about Tara’s studies. He always insists on Chandan coming to his office along with him. He never allows Tara to come to the office. Patel is a typical patriarchal person who thinks “the men in the house were deciding on whether they were going to hunting while the women looked after the cave”. Patel thinks only the men go to the office and the women are looking at the house. From ancient times to modern times, it remains the same. Even if she is a working woman, every woman in society should have completed her housework before going to work.

Tara only gets love and care from her mother, Bharathi. Bharathi is concerned about Tara’s health, and she is feeling guilty inside. She felt so much love towards Tara and was worried about Tara’s future. Tara is longing for Patel’s love and care, but he never shows his love to her. Patel’s only concern about Chandan, his studies, and career, is that he doesn’t care about Tara’s studies or her career. The name Tara, which means ‘STAR,’ wants to shine like a star, but the patriarchal society never allows Tara to shine. If Tara’s own father doesn’t care about her studies and career, then who else cares? Tara and Chandan both had limbs in their legs. When they were born, they had only three legs. Tara had two legs and Chandan had one by birth. Tara had a leg, but society never allowed

Tara to live with it. The family members favour the male heir. Patel asks Dr. Thakkar to transplant Tara's leg to Chandan. After the complicated surgery, they were separated, and now Chandan has two legs and Tara has one leg and the other is made of wood. Patel and his patriarchal mind set would never allow their male heir to be physically challenged, so he did this kind of betrayal to Tara. Patel belongs to the Gujarathi family. In the traditional practice of Patels, they used to drown their girl babies in milk. They were killing the children like this. They use milk to kill their children, revealing it is a typical society. Following the tradition, Patel also committed some kind of inequity towards Tara. Patel never allowed Tara out. He insisted on her helping his mother in the kitchen. Tara is a talented girl. Bharathi only supported her and made her strong. Bharathi protests against the inequality of Tara. Tara is weak physically and mentally. Tara needs kidney transplant surgery. Bharathi wants to donate her own kidney to Tara, but Patel doesn't approve of it. Patel only decides for the women in his family what to do and what not to do.

When Bharathi knits the sweater, Chandan helps his mother with knitting. At that time, Patel saw it and shouted at Chandan for getting involved in knitting. Patel doesn't like this kind of activity. He suggests Chandan should join his office till the result is declared. He considers it a girl's activity and never allows Chandan to do this activity. Who categorises work for men and women? Everyone breathes the same air, everyone eats the same things, so why is there this partiality? Why do women only do the washing, cleaning, cooking, knitting, etc.? Why don't men do this kind of work? Why can't this society accept it? From ancient times to now, women have done these household chores. It is the most pressing question for every woman in Indian society. Chandan is a representative of the new generation of males in Indian society. He doesn't hesitate to help Bharathi with her knitting, which shows the generation gap between Patel and Chandan. He is also concerned about Tara's studies and career. Chandan knows the equality of women and he respects it. Chandan asks Tara to attend college with him. He is also concerned about her career too. He loves Tara more. She is the only best friend of Chandan. They are on the same wavelength.

Bharathi told Chandan about Tara's sacrifice and life in deference to the boy who tells Chandan with reference to Tara, "let her grow up, yes Chandan, the world will tolerate you, the world will accept you, but not her" (CP 348-349). Chandan's remorse for Tara is palpable. The world will accept a male child who is physically challenged, but the world will not accept a female like this. Tara's health was too bad and she died. Tara faces many obstacles and struggles throughout her life. Even her own father doesn't accept her because she is female. From her birth to her death, she was ill treated because of her female gender. Dan suffers with a guilt complex throughout his lifetime. Dan blames himself for Tara's tragic death. He could never lead a peaceful life. Dan feels so much pain and guilt for the rest of his life. He wishes that someday Tara who is among the stars, would forgive him. Dan feels sorry for Tara thus, "Forgive me, Tara. Forgive me for making it my tragedy"(CP 380).

The play *Tara* is undoubtedly a tragedy. The tragedy happened to Tara. She hasn't made any mistakes in her life. The only mistake is she was a girl child that is the only reason she suffered a lot from her birth to death. Dattani portrays gender discrimination and gender inequality throughout the play. In *Tara,* it is observed that gender discrimination as the main theme. In this play, Dattani sketches the agony of a girl child in a male-dominated Indian society.

Reference

Dattani, Mahesh. *Collected Plays*, Penguin, New Delhi, 2000. Print.

CHAPTER TWENTY-THREE

SYMBOLISM OF DARKNESS AND LIGHT IN ENGLISH LITERATURE

V. Swerna Malika,
II MA English,
Edayathangudy G. S. Pillay Arts & Science College (Autonomous),
Nagapattinam.

Symbolism is the idea that things address other things. Darkness and light are two common symbols used in literature. Darkness is a symbol of evil, whereas light represents goodness. The use of light and dark imagery is used to demonstrate the contrast between God and evil. Many writers, like William Shakespeare, Robert Frost, John Milton, F Scott Fitzgerald, Emily Dickinson, and Lord Bryon, have used the imagery of darkness and light in their works. This analysis has focused on some selective works that show the symbolism of darkness and light. In literature, darkness and light mostly represent bad and good things, respectively. It doesn't mean light is always good and dark is bad. The symbolism of darkness and light in literature depends on how the writer uses the motif.

Shakespeare's famous plays, *Macbeth, Romeo and Juliet, Othello* and *Hamlet* have the imagery of darkness and light in different ways. In *Macbeth,* Shakespeare portrayed darkness as a symbol of evilness. He says that it can drive people to madness. It can be observed through the witches; on the night that Duncan is killed. The cloak of darkness covered the deeds of Macbeth and Lady Macbeth. Everything is done in that shroud of darkness. The Instrument of Darkness is one of the symbols of darkness in Macbeth. In Act 1, scene 3 Banquo says,

"But 'tis strange
And oftentimes, to win us to our harm,
The instruments of darkness tell us truths,
Win us with honest trifles, to betrays" (*Macbeth*)

The instrument of darkness is only the witches. Banquo reminds him about the witches and the significance of darkness. He lets him know that instruments of darkness tell the truth. It may or may not happen. He warns Macbeth of the risk of confiding in the witches.

The play *Hamlet* is structured as a revenge tragedy. The play, in a sense, focuses on the character Hamlet. He is always dressed in black throughout the play. These dark outfits symbolise the grief of Hamlet. Shakespeare also conveys that darkness is uncontrollable. Hamlet protecting him shows that he has clashed with his spot. The utilisation of dark language and word choice creates a strange tone in the play, which brings upon the predictable discussion of demise. The very substance of the ambitious is merely the shadow of a dream. It is said by Guildenstern Which means dreams are an indication of aspiration, since desire is just the shadow of a fantasy. Along these lines, the expression can be deciphered as: The essence of overachieving, upwardly achieving individuals is the shade or darkness of their undiscovered dreams. The shadow represents darkness.

In *Othello*, Shakespeare has utilised pictures of light and dark to epitomise the focal subjects of the play. Light addresses guiltlessness, love, and goodness. Desdemona, the fair, saintly spouse of Othello the Moor, exemplifies these qualities in general.

Regardless of her outright commitment and love for Othello, her decency isn't to the point of saving her from the dark and insidious Iago. Darkness comes to represent vindictiveness and treachery, as Iago's desire respects fury, and he moves to annihilate the existences of those he accepts have violated him. With light and dark continually in struggle, Shakespeare uses the pictures to delineate a wide scope of feelings and subjects, from unpleasant to envy, to firm to cherish, to the most disastrous type of disdain. He used the theme of racism, and the great clashes between good and evil are exceptionally conspicuous subjects all through the book, and are, in the long run what prompts the death of Othello and Desdemona. Light versus dark could address only the interracial relationship between Othello and Desdemona, but the profound reader will notice that light addresses immaculateness and truth, whereas the dark addresses secrecy, antagonism, and dread.

Shakespeare used to compare darkness to evil and light to holy in many of his plays. But in the case of *Romeo and Juliet*, the motif of dark and light is expressed in both positive and negative aspects. Romeo and Juliet meet at night in secret.

Away from light steals home my heavy son
And private in his chamber pens himself,
Shuts up his windows, locks fair daylight out,
And makes himself an artificial night (*Romeo and Juliet,* Line *125 - 130*).

This assertion raises the impression of hell and darkness for the audience. Romeo resembles the dark, and he stows away from the light. Romeo is an especially delicate person in the play. He is effectively influenced by his own feelings.

"O, she doth teach the torches to burn bright!
It seems she hangs upon the cheek of night
As a rich Jewel in an Ethiop's ear – Beauty too rich for use, for earth too dear!
So shows a snowy dove trooping with crows
As yonder lady o'er her fellows shows" (*Romeo and Juliet,* Act I. Scene V. 45-50)

This shows that she is a radiant marvel to the crowd and gets the thought. At any rate, her sparkling glory is crucial to Romeo, as he is in the evening, Juliet can lift Romeo's spirits.

In Act 2, Scene 2, Romeo is gazing toward Juliet's window when the light comes on. "What light through yonder window breaks? It is the east, and Juliet is the sun!"

In the play, Montague depicts Romeo as the night. At the point when Romeo sees Juliet, he depicts her as the day. They are from quarrelling houses that disallow them to be together, so they resemble the sun and the moonlight. It is a common conviction among individuals that the moon and the sun can't see one another. "Come night, come Romeo, come thou day in night, for thou wilt lie upon the wings of night" (Act 3, Scene 2, Line 17-18)

Shakespeare has included the night as a cover that safeguards Romeo and Juliet from their families and companions. Night resembles a shroud that permits them to be together without judgment. Along these lines, Juliet is continuously wanting for night to show up rapidly. "More light and light, more dark and dark our woes".

All through the play, light is meddlesome and unwanted, strong and startling; darkness, in any case, is alleviating and uncovering, and permits the play's nominal lovers to get to know each other, to showcase their dreams of affection, and to find their actual selves away from their families. Romeo, driven out for exile in the first part of the day, and Juliet, not needing him to leave her room, both attempts to imagine that it is still evening, and that the light is really darkness.

There are some other works by Shakespeare that have the motifs of light and darkness. Night in Shakespeare is unique in relation to darkness-night is the place where characters are confounded, conflated, and once in a while seized. This motif can be found in the plays *Measure for Measure* or *All's Well That Ends Well, A Midsummer Night's Dream,* and *King Lear. The Tempest* is a play played inside, similar to every one of the late plays, and like them, brimming with equivocal compromise.

In *Paradise Lost*, Milton has portrayed the characters from Hellfire with much more darkness, and he contrasted sublime characters with light. Throughout the epic Paradise Lost, Milton used darkness and light as motifs for contrasting things, such as God and Satan; Hell and Heaven; Angels and Devils. The symbolism of light mostly refers to the things belonging to God, whereas darkness refers to Satan.

Milton further portrayed hellfire as being in "utter darkness" and "far eliminated from God". Adam and Eve are trapped in the middle of the light and darkness. Thus, God is observed as omnipotent and ceaselessly endeavouring to be squashed by the fallen angels, particularly Satan.

Milton's *Paradise Lost Book* III connotes that this light is a heavenly thing. He says that "God is light"

"Hail holy Light, ofspring of Heav'n first-born,
Or of th' Eternal Coeternal beam
May I express thee unblam'd? since God is light."
It is in a real sense coordinated at Light: "Hail, blessed Light"
(*Paradise Lost Book* III 3.1).

However, it isn't simply any light; it is the illumination of God—the light that made all. At the point when Milton presents Light, he gives a few instances of Light's beginnings, suggesting that this sort of light isn't straightforward or visible, like actual light is, and expects the watcher to be genuinely fit for sight. Nonetheless, the peruser could, in any case, confuse this light with ordinary daylight.

"Through utter and through middle darkness borne."
"Long is the way and hard, that out of Hell leads up to light."
"This horror will grow mild, this darkness light."
"Whose Fountain who shall tell? before the Sun,
Before the Heavens thou wert, and at the voice
Of God, as with a Mantle didst invest
The rising world of waters dark and deep." (*Paradise Lost Book* III Line 16)

These are some quotes in *Paradise Lost*, having the symbolism of darkness and light. According to Milton, the initial 55 lines of Book III create a static and obscured outline between the two states, communicating that a couple of things are totally either; According to Milton, there is no light without dark and no dark without light, but most of the time he portrayed light as a new beginning, a holy thing, God's power, bright Heaven, and other positive things in *Paradise Lost*.

In the sonnet, "When I Consider How My Light is Spent," Milton complains that he has become blind even before half of his life has passed in this world. It is also called *"On HisBlindness"*. He believes that his poetic talent is useless to him. Furthermore, he thinks that God will rebuke him when he returns to him for not making proper use of the gift endowed by God. He asks God if he expects him to write noble poetry when he has made him blind. Milton mourns that he is losing his sight when he is scarcely part of the way through life, with quite a bit of his significant work still to be finished. How might he finish his work, which God has given him the ability to do and which God anticipates that he should finish, assuming he is denied his sight? He poses the inquiry to himself, regardless of whether God anticipates that he should work in any event, when he has gone totally visually impaired? Persistently, he responds to himself: God doesn't need work or gift from humanity since God is a ruler.

"When I consider how my light is spent,
Ere half my days, in this dark world and wide,
And that one Talent which is death to hide
Lodged with me useless, though my Soul more bent
To serve therewith my Maker, and present
My true account, lest he returning chide." (*"On His Blindness"*
Line 1-8)

Milton has utilised an illustration to contrast his vision with a light source that could run out, similar to an older style lamp that consumes its oil. He utilises one more allegory to contrast his absence of vision with an envisioned world that doesn't have light. The expression "this dark world and wide" is additionally an illustration of similar-sounding word usage. In this sonnet, Milton is extremely miserable and depressed because he turned out to be totally blind when he was in his forty-fourth year. He is left alone in this dark and huge world, and this condition strengthens a visually impaired man's sensation of helplessness.

Robert Frost was most likely one of America's cherished present-day poets, and his sonnets contain many pictures of light and dark. He was a writer of the human condition. His expectation was to concentrate his attention on life. Life is displayed in Frost's sonnets to contain numerous parts of darkness, which frequently appear to be connected in a progression of melancholies of the human soul. Life, too, is at times unnerving, filling men with dread and vulnerability. An infinite series of things appears to assault the actual vitals of man's satisfaction, and on occasion the infinite idea of the assault would imply man's definitive loss. This exposition manages a few of these dark components in Frost's verse, against which all of humankind should wage a continuing fight. There are many poems by Frost expressing the imagery of dark, night, and light. "Stopping by Woods on a Snowy Evening" is one of the famous poems by Frost. "The darkest evening of the year." "The woods are lovely, dark and deep." It suggests a feeling of experience and fascination with risk—the 'darkness' and 'profundity' of the forest. Maybe the speaker needs to encounter new things and spots, but his obligations—his work, his family—hold him back from going off on dark and risky adventures.

*"Acquainted with the Night"*The night is a representation of darkness, which can be deciphered as misery, wretchedness, enduring or despair. The storyteller is familiar with these sensations of despair in light of the dejection communicated all through the sonnet. Regardless of whether it's with regard to the absence of light. However, there's something else to the dark and light of this sonnet than meets the eye. This sonnet can be perused as a similitude of the dark gloom. However, the radiance of the moon actually comes to pass through the lights of the city and

mankind, an image of hope.

In Frost's poems, "Design" is frequently considered to be Frost's dark reaction to the traditional contention from which it derives, the contention for a clever, generous God. To this end, a few instructors avoid this strong sonnet, trusting it to be built against the presence of this great God. Subjects like the presence of God. 'Design' has no exception. His customary work is a simile for the storyteller, in his own particular manner, attempting to control and comprehend nature's confusion.

In the sonnet "Come In," Frost's imagery by means of birds, and light, symbolism of the woods, and comparisons, line breaks, rhyme, and generally speaking, tragic tone, outlines the darkness of his considerations, feelings, and thoughts. In "Too dark in the woods for a bird"*(line 5)*,he utilises the imagery of darkness to convey that even birds can't live in the woods in view of the presence of darkness. "The last of the light of the sun",

In the above lines, light stands for hope. Throughout this poem, he has used light and dark as contrary things. Frost oftentimes showed a human requirement for retreat from life's abusiveness; however, never did he demonstrate escape. He considered escape a demonstration of conclusion, a demonstration that could never be scattered. A man should adapt to his reality. He should not submit to the call of the obscure woods. While adapting to life's difficulties demonstrates insufficient, man should gain proficiency with the worth of acceptance. When a man considers himself to be companionless, or when genuine correspondence among him has been hampered, an excess of reflection prompts a feeling of distance from the world and a longing to get away from the world's influence. Even nature itself is scary. He depicts nature as severe and barbarous, savage. A man should control his anxieties towards the regular world by practicing mental fortitude. However, regular powers are antagonistic; they don't carry on a plan of malevolence. Nature is similarly fit to help man, breaking his darkness with pictures of light and trust like stars, the moon, and the sun. These pictures highlight the truth of truth, the presence of a justification behind living, for battling against life's harshness. In this way, Frost didn't permit the dark to go whole in his sonnets. He wanted truth to be seen and perceived as the main power fit for dissipating the shadow of human obliviousness and human gloom, empowering man to get by in a milieu of darkness. It is believed that this thesis will provide the peruser with a significant, all-around regularly disregarded side of Robert Frost's verse that should be perceived assuming Frost is to be completely valued.

Byron's "Darkness", It serves as an early warning of the developing divergence in Byron's time and a figure of what will happen to the planet if humanity does not change.

The speaker dreams a horrendous dream in which humankind destroys itself after the sun burns out and leaves the world without light. Frantic and starving in a timeless evening, the overcomes of this debacle very quickly go to murder and barbarianism. The genuine frightfulness of these end times, the sonnet suggests, isn't simply the strict darkness of a dark world. It's the allegorical darkness inside individuals' spirits: the eagerness, brutality, and narrow-mindedness prowling just beneath socialised surfaces, prepared to arise the second that individuals feel that their own endurance is undermined.

I had a dream, which was not all a dream.
The bright sun was extinguish'd, and the stars
Did wander darkling in the eternal space,
Rayless, and pathless, and the icy earth
Swung blind and blackening in the moonless air. ("Darkness" Line 1-5)

The moon, their mistress, had expir'd before;
The winds were wither'd in the stagnant air,
And the clouds perish'd; Darkness had no need
Of aid from them—She was the Universe. ("Darkness" Line 79-82)

This poem came under the theme of darkness. Byron's speaker cautions against the developing imbalance that he perceives in his time and makes forecasts concerning what will occur, assuming nothing changes. Byron's speaker investigates the future, and what he sees isn't generally lovely. The sun, stars, and moon are completely suppressed, and the people of Earth are left wandering aimlessly. They are ill-fated to live in darkness because of their past activities.

Scott Fitzgerald uses a contrast of light and dark imagery and distinct language to outline the quest for bliss and the lack of ethics that power-hungry individuals experience inside the privileged in *The Great Gatsby.* Light is used to address idealism and dreams. A thumbs up close to the completion of a dock figures recognisably in the novel as an aid to the unique American dream. In a dark storm cellar, Meyer Wolfsheim, a player, first becomes familiar with the narrator of the novel. In this way, Wolfsheim and the darkness from which he emerges address insatiability, contamination, and the unwanted side of the city. "Gatsby believed in the green light, the orgiastic future that year by year recedes before us" (21).

The green light that Fitzgerald examines appears as though it were Gatsby's craving to one day go with Daisy. Gatsby acknowledged that he could achieve being with Daisy and attempted continually to intrigue her throughout the novel, as the green light is ceaselessly depicted as being scarcely out of Gatsby's reach across the lake. *"The valley of ashes is bounded on one side by a small foul river" (24).*

Fitzgerald utilises the valley of ashes to represent Tom's unfaithfulness and the deficiency of steadfastness to Daisy for his own power-hungry plans. The valley of remains has a dark and dreary undertone, addressing and anticipating the misery of this issue with Myrtle. This undertaking is important for Tom's quest for bliss and his endeavour to gain more power in his relationship. *The Great Gatsby*, light is meaningful of the uncanny appreciation of Jay Gatsby's riches and influence, enlightening the glow and lucidity it brings as well as its detachment and triviality. Light is ever-present all through the novel, reflecting changes from dark, violent times to more splendid, happier ones.

*"We grow accustomed to the dark"*is a poem about the unsettling aspects of life, such as facing the future with little idea of how to proceed, or strolling into the night with no light to guide life.For somebody who seldom blended with the rest of the world, she sure figured out how to pick a subject we can all connect with, regardless of whether we aren't in a real sense terrified of the dark. *"We grow accustomed to the Dark – When Light is put away l" (Poem)*

The primary line of the sonnet furthermore outfits the poem with its guideline subject: the way the eyes adapt to the murkiness. As the characters conform to thc sadness of life and the assessment of the 'night' that is destruction.

"There's a certainSlantof *light,"*It is a sonnet having imagery of light. It's a meditation on sadness—where it comes from, what it looks like, and what it means for the psyche, soul, and, surprisingly, the scene. All in all, seeing this chilly day causes the speaker to feel down, despondent, and choked. The sonnet proceeds to investigate the beginnings and impacts of this strange, despairing inclination, which the sonnet at last infers is an unavoidable piece of being human. This sonnet revolves around the way that sunlight in the winter is abusive and burdens us, causing us to feel low, troubled, as though visited by a 'Heaven Hurt'.

This study aims at analysing a few works in literature with the imagery of darkness and light. We cannot come to the conclusion that darkness is only used to represent negative things and light is for positive things. In literature, we can see so many writers have their own opinion about darkness and light. Most of them portrayed darkness as an evil thing and light as a good one. It is totally up to the writers how they express the motifs of dark and light. Darkness is not something to be feared. As a human being, everyone has a real side as well as a shadow side. We are both light and dark; suppressing either one unbalances us. Light cannot be exposed without darkness. It doesn't exclude anyone from that. Dark and light are typically compared with black and white, but it may create some illusion that black is a symbol of evil, as in black cat, black tragedy, black mark. This thought leads to colour discrimination.

Dark and light, or black and white, are contrary things, as day and night are equally valuable.

Reference

Andrews, J. F. "DEARLY Bought Revenge: Samson Agonistes, *Hamlet*". *Milton Studies*

Published By: Penn State University Press, 1979, Page. No. 81–107. Print.

https://www.enotes.com/homework-help/provide-the-setting-and-context-of-the-following-531809. Accessed 18 Feb. 2022.

Gordon, Todd. Kissel, Adam ed. "Lord Byron's Poems "Darkness" Summary and Analysis". Grade Saver, 31 December 2011 Web. 19 February 2022.

Howard, James. "We grow accustomed to the Dark." LitCharts. LitCharts LLC, 4 Nov 2020. Web. 8 Feb 2022.

Lewis, C. S. A preface to paradise lost A preface to paradise lost. New York, NewYork: HarperAudio, 2022. Print.

Milton: Prose Works, Poetical Works (ed. 1843)

"Robert Frost Quotes." BrainyQuote.com. BrainyMedia Inc, 2022. 18 February 2022. https://www.brainyquote.com/quotes/robert_frost_151806

CHAPTER TWENTY-FOUR

Uniqueness of Elizabeth Bennet in Jane Austen's "Pride and Prejudice"

L.B. Thamil Yazhini,
BA-English (2018 - 2022),
Bon Secours College for Women,
Thanjavur.

Jane Austen was an English novelist who was born in 1775. Other works of her are *Sense and Sensibility*, *Mansfield Park*, *Emma*, *Northanger Abbey* and *Persuasion*. The most popular and the notable work is *Pride and Prejudice*. She had a highbrow in portraying the characters well in the novel. She is such a great novelist. Even now her novels are celebrated by many literary scholars.

- That young lady had a talent for describing the involvements and feelings and characters of ordinary life, which is to me the most wonderful I ever met with. The big Bow-Wow strain I can do myself like any now going; but the exquisite touch,

> which renders ordinary commonplace things and characters interesting from the truth of the description, and the sentiment, is denied to me. What a pity such a gifted creature died so early! – (Sir Walter Scott)

The main theme of the novel is love and its subthemes are social rank, gender roles, and family. Nevertheless, this research study aims to manifest Elizabeth Bennet, a maverick young lady! who just allured everyone by her spectacular perspectives and her charismatic personality through her doers in the novel. Jane Austen has projected herself through Elizabeth Bennet.

Her uprightness, decorum and shrewdness empower her to overcome the acrimony that pervade during the nineteenth century. "One of the five heroines of nineteenth century literature" – (Saintsbury), he also said that if she had been alive, he would have married her.

Elizabeth also called as "Lizzy" by her friends and family, the second daughter of Bennet family. She is one of the most commendable female characters. She is not demure and too garrulous. She strives hard to express her ipseity in the restricted society. Although women do have more rights because hitherto there is a struggle for full equality! Elizabeth wants to change the conventional thinking of marriage. She doesn't like to constrain herself. She has aplomb. "I hate to hear you talk about all women as if they were fine ladies instead of rational creatures. None of us want to be in calm waters of all our lives" – (Jane Austen, Persuasion).

She doesn't revere people and things just because society reveres them. She has always contemplated over people, things and acted according to her own conscience. She is not a snobbish woman and disrespects the social norms and customs. In fact, she has high human value and naturally, bestowed with sagacity, thinking independently of her family, friends and neighbors.

Caroline Bingley, a minor antagonist is the younger sister of Mr. Charles Bingley and Louisa Hurst. She invites Jane Bennet to stay at Netherfield. Actually, Jane doesn't want to leave Elizabeth. Her mother Mrs. Bennet is a boisterous and a doltish woman. Her only aim is to see all her daughters to be married to with sumptuous person. She feels ecstatic and persuaded Jane to mount on horseback so that she has to stay all night if it rains. Unfortunately, a downpour continues that whole night! So, she feels unwell. She couldn't recuperate from that hardship. She is completely ill. After receiving the tidings from Jane, Elizabeth feels worried. She is very closer to her elder sister than all other younger ones. The camaraderie between Jane and Elizabeth was quite astonishing. She has no carriage and she is not an equestrienne. Walking is her only alternative. Her mother shouts at her. But she is unswerving on her decision to see Jane by walk. "The distance is nothing when one has a motive, only three miles" (*Pride and Prejudice*, 30).

She reaches Netherfield after facing so many complications. It's really been an arduous journey to her. She looks hideous. This shows that Lizzy's assiduous nature that how much she cares, loves her sister and she is too determined about her decision. Once the decision is indefatigable and find the motive and purpose in life, certainly it can be accomplished what the dream of. This teaches resilient too. The determination of Elizabeth to care Jane by walk which first rose from the intense love for her sister. "When we love, we always strive to become better than we are, when we strive to become better than we are, everything around us becomes better too" – (Paulo Coelho, Alchemist).

When one loves truly someone or loves to do something, he diligently works for it. And that's what enlighten loved one's life and which naturally brings the feeling of exuberance in life becomes better, much better.

Elizabeth Bennet is a keen-witted woman. She could apprehend the circumstances and the people well. When Caroline Bingley informs Jane of her brother's plan to marry Georgiana Darcy, Darcy's sister. Jane at once trusts it. Elizabeth anyhow, knows the true disposition of Caroline Bingley such a hauteur and a jealously woman. Lizzy tells her sister Jane that the whole thing is a part of subterfuge planned by Caroline to marry Mr. Darcy. She knows Mr. Collins to be a nefarious moron from the first letter he has written to the Bennet's family.

At the very first encounter Elizabeth comprehends the personality of Lady Catherine de Bourgh who is Mr. Darcy's aunt and the well-wisher to Mr. Collins and his wife is a wealthy widow woman with the disposition of superciliousness. Elizabeth is reasonably gratified of her discernment. In case of some occasions her discernment fails and where her realization occurred. She is inept of savviness of some complex characters. She prejudices Mr. Darcy that he is a conceited and an unamiable person. She has stated that Mr. Darcy as, "There is, I believe in every disposition a tendency to some particular evil a natural defect, which not even the best education can overcome" (Pride and Prejudice, 53).

However, her first impression of Mr. Darcy is tolerable but not handsome enough, Elizabeth's pride is profoundly maimed by Darcy's rancor words. After sometimes, she meets Mr. George Wickham who speaks ill of Darcy. Wickham makes scurrilous remarks on him. She believes all that he said. Her abhorrence of Darcy augmented. When she comes to know about the counterfeit of Wickham and his averment on Darcy is false. She tells about the malevolence of Wickham to Jane but she couldn't trust that. "What a stroke was this for poor Jane! Who would willingly have gone through the world without believing that so much wickedness existed in the whole race of mankind, as was here collected in one individual" (*Pride and Prejudice*, 195).

Elizabeth is brimmed with repugnance at her own blind prejudice against Darcy. She snivels out and she couldn't bear the agony. She grows completely abashed of herself.

- "How despicably have I acted!" She cried; "I, who have prided myself on my discernment! I, who have valued myself on my abilities! Who have often disdained the generous candor of my sister, and gratified my vanity in useless or [blamable] distrust How humiliating is this discovery! (*Pride and Prejudice*, 182)

Yes, sometimes, it is nature to commit mistakes in life. Of course, that's human nature need not to be an impeccable fellow all the time. When have the capable of mind and heart to accept and rectify the mistakes, life would certainly become bliss. This is a moment of verity for Elizabeth, a moment of fervent self-realization. At last, she realizes her idiocy after so many bewilderments.

Elizabeth has a splendid view on marriage. According to her, if one has to be endowed with a connubial status, love would be their top most priority. Her dearest comrade Charlotte, who marries Mr. Collins only to lead an opulent lifestyle, she does not love him and even she is skeptical to believe that "Love" is an indispensable for to lead a triumphant marriage. Her younger sister Lydia Bennet is an impetuous and temerarious young lady. Despite the fact that the disposition of Lydia has appeared originally an innocuous and a hilarious one but her elopement with Mr. Wickham shows that her egotistical conduct could have led to a somber repercussion. She runs away with him because she gets enmeshed by his beguiling appearance.

All that glisters is not gold;
Often have you
Heard that told:
Many a man his
Life hath sold
But my outside
To behold
Glided tombs do
Worms enfold. (*The Merchant of Venice* ActII Scene VII)

Elizabeth has a splendid opinion on life and marriage. She firmly believes that 'marriage is more about than love the economic statuses. Love is beyond the caste, complexion and the social hierarchy. She loves Darcy a lot. Their love is true. After tackled so many impediments and baffled situations, Darcy and Elizabeth get reconciled. The kinship between Elizabeth Bennet and Mr. Darcy is demonstrated as the state of euphoria can be attained if both of them marry for true love.

Austen throughout her novel exemplifies the societal state of the nineteenth century in England with cognizance of the social issues that affect the society, where marriage is based on economical status and social class rather than amity and love. She wants to eradicate the conventional thinking about marriage during her period. She authenticates that the wealth, caste could give raise to the chagrin, dejection and segregation. Elizabeth Bennet is a role model for all women. She is one of the most effervescent female literary characters ever written. She strongly demurs the stereotypes related to gender, social and cultural norms. She remained as the dynamic protagonist. Each and every feature and approach of her must be learnt and followed by all women.

Reference

Austen, Jane, *Pride and Prejudice*, Penguin Classics Reprint, 1994.

Austen, Jane, *Persuasion*: A Jane Austen's Classic Novel, 200th Anniversary Collection Edition, 2021.

Coelho, Paulo, *The Alchemist*. London, England: Thorsons,1995.

George Allen, *Illustrations by Hugh Thomson*, Peacock edition, 1895.

Scott, Walter, *The Journal of Sir Walter Scott. Anderson,* W.E.K. Edinburgh: Canongate, ISBN 0862418283. OCLC 40905767,1998.

Shakespeare, William, and W M. Merchant. *The Merchant of Venice*. Harmondsworth, Middlesex: Penguin Books, 1967.

CHAPTER TWENTY-FIVE

Analytical Study on Gender Discrimination in Virginia Woolf's "To the Lighthouse" and Mahesh Dattani's "Tara"

Thasneem. S,
II M.A. English,
Edayathangudy G. S. Pillay Arts and Science College (Autonomous),
Nagapattinam.

Attempt of this research study is all about gender discrimination, which is done by the men's domination that is always degrading women. Virginia Woolf's *To the Lighthouse* and Mahesh Dattani's *Tara* are considered the best known works to deal with gender discrimination.

Virginia Woolf was an English writer. She is considered one of the most important modernists in 20th-century literature. She was born on the 25th January 1882 in London and died on the 28th March 1941 in London. She was a prolific writer of essays, diaries, letters, and biographies. *To the Lighthouse* is the best novel published in 1927. On the other hand, Mahesh Dattani is not only a playwright but also an actor and director. His *Tara* is known for its patriarchal system.

To the Lighthouse by Virginia Woolf is a great novel. It centres on Ramsay's family and their visits to the Isle of Skye in Scotland. Ramsay is a philosophical person, and his wife is a pious woman. They have eight children. In this novel, one guest character arrives as an admirer of Mr. Ramsay named Charles Tansley, who is a narrow-minded person and always thought that women are not allowed to do painting and writing. It means that women are not eligible for that; they only deserve to be housekeepers. Their predictions and thoughts are totally wrong. Because women are not eligible for everything they want to do on their own volition. But here Charles Tansley said that a woman doesn't do anything they like. As the same thing can be observed in another work, *Tara* by Mahesh Dattani, Patel is the father of Tara and Chandan, who is always degrading women. He doesn't care for his daughter which can be understood through his actions and words, but he encourages his son Chandan, who is the male child of the family. Chandan and Tara are conjoined twins, so they were operated on to separate. When they were born, they had only three legs. Two of them belonged to Tara, but Patel decides to give one of Tara's one leg to Chandan. Patel thought that a girl child doesn't need two legs because she is not going to achieve nor do anything meaningful in the future because she is a girl and will never be allowed to achieve anything. She is only used to doing household work under a man's domination. She is not allowed to go out. She is simply seen as a slave, as per the patriarchal view. He believes that those women exist solely to care for the family and the food department. They are not born to do only domestic work. They too have emotions, dreams, and ambitions like men. Their education and creativity levels are better than men's. Men think that women are physically weaker than they are. But in reality, they are the strongest people compared to men. Women are mentally and physically stronger than men. They could tackle every hard phase and they knew how to go through the contexts. So both works show the same thing about gender discrimination. Even though society is also not supporting women's education or whatever else they do. They are only too ready to backbite badly about women's and underestimate their hard work. They are going on slandering women. So you people, please stop criticising them and change the mentality towards them. They are women, not cowards. Gender discrimination is a major issue in India. So people should stop this action. It may affect the upcoming generations, and it will continue. This may offend women who are trying to reach a good position in life. Say no to gender discrimination.

Gender discrimination is when there are unfair rights between males and females. It differs because of their gender roles, which ultimately lead to unequal treatment in life. Gender discrimination has been around for many centuries. Education can bring about a change in this mindset because educated people will less likely partake in gender discrimination. Further, poverty is also another reason which is interlinked in a way. It is the root cause in many places because the economic dependence remains on the male counterparts mostly. Thus, women suffer a lot from it for the same reason. They never get out of this and stay financially dependent on men. Furthermore, the patriarchal setup in the society plays a big role. In this setup, the male dominates almost every aspect of life. Thus, they consider themselves to be superior to others. This way, a lot of violence and injustice are meted out against women. Thus, when there is a gender considered to be superior, it becomes difficult for everyone to enjoy equal opportunities. Gender discrimination has a deep impact on society as a whole. It affects the entire society, not just a small portion of it. First of all, it impacts children as they fall prey to gender stereotypes at a young age. It impacts young people because it impacts their behavior, study choices, ambitions, attitudes and more.

Many girls do not participate in sports, and women are more likely than men to be physically abused. Gender discrimination affects adults because there is a gender pay gap in the working class. Men are paid more than women for doing the same work. So, why do people judge people based on their gender? Discrimination is defined as judging people based on how they look, act, and dress, as well as their age, religion, race, or gender. Discrimination starts in the mind and then becomes a natural habit that humans have in their everyday lives.

Discrimination is not only a topic on which everyone is concerned; it is also a serious issue that primarily affects women. Why is discrimination directed towards women? Discrimination against women is not just discrimination against a person; it is discrimination against families as well. Women don't have the right to freely choose their career; they are obliged to accept work according to what is known as traditional women's work. Women don't have the full right to benefit from the job's services.

Governments should provide specific measures against violence against women in their workplaces. Women have assumed the roles of mother, housewife, and nurturer; they are stereotyped to work at home, cook, and care for children. However, when it comes to women working outside the home, they are viewed as self-centered and selfish, despite the fact that some women are better and more capable of reaching higher levels in the work field than men; is this accepted? In addition, women do the same jobs as men but receive lower wages. When it comes to payment in the work field, they look at the gender of the person rather than at the number of hours they spend working or at the type of work they do. Strides have certainly been made to improve the workplace for women, but their potential still goes largely untapped. To begin with, many women are the sole source of financial support for themselves or their families. Furthermore, the jobs that women mainly got are in what now consider traditionally women's work, such as nurses or sectaries. Having a daughter brings sadness to some families as they know the struggle their daughters will face. Compared to males, their lives are much harder as the experience of being a female is more of a burden than anything else. There is no day off being a woman in a household. Whether being a sister, daughter, daughter-in-law or mother-in-law, there is always a task assigned to you. However, claiming woman's education doesn't only apply to one sex or the other. It applies to both sexes, but the majority of the time it has proved to be different for women. It is raised to believe that the most important job that must withhold is being a mother and raising a family. While men are expected to be the head of the household and obtain jobs within different industries of their choosing, Women are considered the weaker sex and are left to do things like housework and take care of children instead of working out in the fields. Women should have the same opportunities as men to get a job and be given the same pay. Women are forced to take jobs that hadn't been taken by men, such as school teachers. The minority may all belong to the same group, but yet there are many categories within that group that also deal with more than one form of oppression. In the article, the author makes valid points about the daily struggles of being a woman in society but also shines light on the issue that she also faces other forms of oppression because of her skin colour. Since the beginning of time, women have had different roles than men. Women have been the ones to take care of the family in the home, and men have been the ones to take care of the financial needs. Social media plays a massive role in what it means to be a woman, but especially what it means to be a so-called good mother.

All around the world, discrimination exists. Religion, race, sexuality, and gender are characteristics that cause unequal treatment of people. A developed country may overcome different social obstacles than a developing country, but certain issues are critical on an international scale. Women's inequality in society is still a prevalent issue that should be addressed. In reality not every marriage is a functional one. Society plays a huge role in the repression that is enforced in marriage. Individuals are more accepting of marriage now and understand that every person does not necessarily want to marry but is unhappy and feels trapped. Perhaps in "The Story of an Hour" and "The Yellow Wallpaper", the husbands might love their wives and the feeling might be mutual, but since it all took place in a different time period where society harshly criticizes women for not being married or for leaving the marriage they are in.

This study concludes with the analytical view that gender discrimination exists in *To the Lighthouse* and *Tara*. Gender discrimination must be checked at every stage so that no person should be denied a chance to learn and grow. Everyone, no matter whether male or female, must get a start in life in terms of education.

Reference

Dattani, Mahesh. "Tara". *Collected Plays*. New Delhi: Penguin Books, 2000.

Pant, Tanu, and R K. Dhawan. *The Plays of Mahesh Dattani, a Critical Response*. New Delhi: Prestige Books, 2005. Print.

Woolf, Virginia. *To the Lighthouse*. London: Marshall Cavendish, 1988. Print.

CHAPTER TWENTY-SIX

"The Dreams of Tipu Sultan": An Overview

K.A.Yazhini,
MA English (2020-2022),
Edayathangudy G. S. Pillay Arts & Science College
(Autonomous),
Nagapattinam.

Girish Karnad was born on May 19, 1938, in Mathern, Maharashtra. Girish Karnad has become one of India's brightest shining stars, earning international praise as a playwright, poet, actor, director, critic, and translator. As a young man studying at Karnataka University, Dharwar, where he earned a Bachelor of Arts degree in Mathematics and Statistics in 1958, Karnad dreamed of earning international literary fame, but he thought that he would do so by writing in English. Upon graduation, he went to England and studied at Oxford; where he earned a Rhodes scholarship and went on to receive a Master of Arts degree in philosophy, politics, and economics. He would eventually achieve the international fame he had dreamed of, but not for his English poetry. Instead, Karnad would earn his reputation through decades of consistent literary output on his native soil.

His first play, Yayati (1961), was written neither in English nor in his mother tongue, Konkani. Instead, it was composed in his adopted language, Kannada. Karnad received many awards, including the Mysore State Award for Yayathi (1962), The Government of Mysore Rajyotsava Award (1970), The Sangeet Natak Academy (National Academy of the Performing Arts) Award for playwriting (1972), the 'Writer of the Year' Award from Granthaloka Journal of the Book Trade for Taledanda (1990), The Padma Bhushan Award (1992) and The Sahitya Academy Award for Taledanda (1994).

The story follows the last days as well as the historic moments in the life of the ruler of Mysore, Tipu Sultan, through the eyes of an Indian court historian, Mir Hussain Ali Khan Kirmani, and a British oriental scholar, Colin Mackenzie.

The play is taken from the historical account of Tipu Sultan, who fought against the British domination of India. The play is based on the following events in Indian history about the ruler, Tipu Sultan, and his enmity towards the British.

The English fought four Anglo-Mysore wars against Tipu Sultan to defeat him and gain control over the Mysore kingdom, as Tipu did not agree to cede to the British demands like the Nizams and Marathas.

The British started their operations against Srirangapatna starting early in 1792. The English army marched against the fort and arrived at the sight of the fortress on the 16th of February 1792. On the same night, the operations started, and the English pushed Tipu's force to the fort and captured this entire island except the fort. Helplessly, Tipu proposed the peace treaty and accepted the terms dictated by Lord Cornwallis. They signed the treaty on February 23rd, 1792. As per the treaty, Tipu agreed to surrender half of his territory to the English and pay three crores thirty lakhs of rupees as war indemnity to the English.

Since he could not pay the war indemnity in full, he accepted to send his second and third sons, namely Abdul Khaliq and Maiz-Uddin, aged 10 and 8 respectively, as hostages till he could pay the war indemnity. He paid the balance amount after two years and received his sons in 1794 A.D. at Devanahalli.

After the third Mysore war, Tipu Sultan sent envoys to Persia, France, and Afghanistan to seek help from them in fighting against the English. He contacted Napoleon Bonaparte also. Though he accepted to help Tipu against the English because of his failure against the English, he could not keep his word. He planned a holy war against the English along with Afghanistan. This failed because of the timely action of Wellesley.

Considering these strategies of Tipu Sultan, Wellesley wrote a letter to Tipu Sultan on the 8th of November 1798 A.D. complaining that Tipu was working against the treaty of Srirangapatna. And he suggested resolving the problems through discussion. Wellesley's suggestions were ignored by Tipu. And so the English declared a war against Tipu Sultan.

On 4thMay, 1799 A.D., Srirangapatna was seized by the English after killing Tipu Sultan in the fourth Mysore war.

Girish Karnad uses this historical account in his play "DREAMS OF TIPU SULTAN" with the incorporation of the dream allegory to portray the downfall of Tipu Sultan and leaves the interpretations to the readers and audience.

In *The Dreams of Tipu Sultan,* he uses the concept of dreams to indicate the downfall of Tipu Sultan through his dreams. The dreams of Tipu Sultan can be interpreted as symbols or an indication that focus on his downfall in the future. The Dream Book (Khwab-Nama) was looted from Seringapatam along with other books. The book was not in the library or the royal library in Seringapatam. It was discovered hidden in the bed chamber of Tipu Sultan's palace, Lal Mahal, the ruin of which can be seen today in front of the Sri Ranganatha Swamy Temple. That nobody saw the book or had an occasion to read it. He kept it so well hidden that even his personal servant and body guard couldn't locate it. What makes this book unique is that it can give us a clear and unambiguous portrait of the man that Tipu was, his inner conflict, and his ambition. His dream was recorded in flawless Persian, a tribute to the language skills of the Sultan. Most of the dreams are about his conflicts with the British and the volatile political situation of the times. The dreams tell us that Tipu was a human like anyone like us and that the hectic life he lived was reflected in his dreams too. The dreams are an inner reflection of his personality and a mirror to his unconscious self. The dreams are made with own handwriting and reflect his innermost thoughts.

Habibullah, the munshi of the Sultan, was present at the time the manuscript was discovered. But he too had only heard of the dreams and had never seen them. On April 23rd, 1805, this book was presented in the name of the Marquis of Wellesley to Hugh Inglis, Chairman of the Court of Directors of the East India Company, by Major Alexander Beatson. A copy of this book is available in the Biblitheque National of Paris which was made for it in 1822.

The dreams and other notes in the book were recorded on the first thirty-two pages and again on eleven pages toward the end of it. In between, a large number of pages are left blank. The size of the register is 7 inches by 51 inches. The dreams cover thirteen years of his reign from 1785-1798.

After the death of Tipu Sultan on May 4th, 1799, his library was taken away to England and is now part of the libraries at Cambridge and Oxford, as well as the Indian Office Library in London and the Asiatic Society in Calcutta. Most of these dreams are devoted to driving the British out of India and defeating the Nizam.

Karnad's has only four dreams mentioned in the play. And all the dreams are political allegories. But in history, Tipu had recorded 37 dreams in his dreams book (Khwab-nama), which was found by Colonel Patrick and these were recorded between the years 1785-1798.

When they saw a dairy, they saw an odd little book, a pleasantly inconsequential conversation piece. This dream book was presented as an ideal gift to the Chairman of the Honorable East India Company in April 1800 on behalf of Marquis Wellesley.

In history, the dreams themselves, thirty seven in all, date from April 1786 to January 16th, 1799, leading historians to believe that the book was compiled over that entire period. But close analysis of its contents has now revealed that the register is directly connected to the final year of Tipu's life and that it dates from no earlier than 1795.

Tipu first dream in the play is dream 9 of his dream book in history. His first dream came on the 3rd day of month of Thamari, the last night of the month of Ramzan, followed the next morning by IDD in the year of Dalw, 1213, the birth of the prophet. He was returning with his army from Farrukh, near Salamabad, when he had the following dream.

Karnad's, second is to come up with the first dream. In history, the second dream was dream 10 out of his 37 dreams. In this, Tipu saw two old men with long beards, in flowing silk gowns, approaching them. Besides them are two elephants and several footmen carrying spears and guns.

The third dream in the play "The Woman in the Man's Dress" is dream XIII out of his 37 dreams. This dream came on the sixth day of the Khusrawi month in the year of Busd, as he was preparing for a night attack on the Maratha armies with 300 men under general Hari Pant Phadke at Shahnur near Devgiri. He had a dream. A young man in a turban like a Maratha enters. A handsome man, fair skinned and light-eyed, a female voice approached him.

Further Haider said he had no arms. English is stranger now and scared of them and think like a trader. But Tipu says he will not let them. He will restore his father's limbs and arms and his dream left out.

The last dream in the play is victory over the British. Kirmani remembers it vividly. But the crucial detail still eludes him. Sultan was staying in the caravanserai on the northern ramparts. He'd been there for a couple of days, with the soldiers, watching the English noose tighten. It was sweltering hot, so they began to pray for a downpour. For them, the moats would have been flooded and the English attack delayed. But the cloud had hung ominously, inert, neutral. We were half way through our lunch, our sweat streaming into our plates, when the skies exploded. The English had launched their assault. The Sultan washed his finger and got up. He buckled on his sword belt, took out an envelope from his pocket, sealed it and gave it to me. 'Keep it till I come back,' he said. He mumbled a prayer and left. Kirmani forgot about the letter. The next day, he found it in his pocket. He broke the seal and inside was a piece of paper on which he had recorded his last dream.

Tipu was killed on the 4th of May, 1799. In a fraction of a second after identifying the Sultan's dead body, the wailing of a female is heard in the far distance. The British were surprised at how the ladies of the palace knew so soon. The palace was a mile away, 'some secret signal'. The wailing gets louder and spreads. The entire city was soon wailing. The wailing of the ladies washed away the dreams of the Sultan. But his last dream was fulfilled after one hundred and fifty years of his death when India got independence from the British.

The subconscious mind is a most remarkable mechanism when it comes to creating dreams. Most people find their dreams an unintelligible mix of hidden meanings and secret symbols because that is the intention of the subconscious mind. It wants no interference from the dreamer's input or meddling with any of its actions.

Girish Karnad, in his play *The Dream of Tipu Sultan,* uses the concept of dreams to indicate the downfall of Tipu Sultan through his dreams. The dreams of Tipu can be interpreted as symbols or an indication which focuses on his downfall in the future and the Marathas as' 'women in men's garb ', i.e., as those who cannot save themselves from the clutches of the British.

The Dreams of Tipu Sultan uses the concept of dreams to indicate the downfall of Tipu Sultan through his dreams. Karnad has described that the dreams as the factual incidents of Tipu's life. In the historical record, he had 37 dreams, but in the Karnad plays, only four dreams are discussed. And all the dreams are political allegories and facts. The Dreams book (Khwab-nama), his only soul mate was found by Colonel Patrilk and recorded between the years 1785-1798. All of his dreams were to drive out the British from the native land of India to the far off sea of land. His final wish was realised one hundred and fifty years after his death.

Reference

Hasan, Mohibbul. "The Last War with the English: *The fall of Seringapatam*", in *History of Tipu Sultan*, Delhi: Aakar Books, 2017.

Karnad, Girish. T*he Dreams of Tipu Sultan: Bali : the Sacrifice : Two Plays*. New Delhi: Oxford University Press, 2004. Print.

Kumar, Krishnamurthy. "*The Dreams of Tipu Sultan at Mysore*" in Girish Karnad's Plays Performance and Critical Perspectives, (ed.), Tutun Murkherjee, 2008.

CHAPTER TWENTY-SEVEN

HUMANISTIC APPROACHES IN "THE BLUE UMBRELLA" BY RUSKIN BOND

M. Yuvarani &
E. Ganga,
II MA English, Government College for Women (Autonomous), Kumbakonam.

The Blue Umbrella is a beautiful story about a mountain girl, Binya, and her adventures with a bright blue silk umbrella. But in deep observation, the story revolves around human emotions. Bond portrays the emotions in an elegant style. He reveals emotions like happiness, sadness, disappointment, pain, anger, greed, pride, jealousy, sacrifice, and remorse. In his little novella, he showed most of the common emotions faced in life.

Without the Himalayas, there is no Ruskin, and the Himalayas would not have another admirer like him. First, he introduces the girl to two cows, Neelu and Gori. Also, he describes the beauty of the Garhwal, the mountains in the Himalayas. Whoever is attached to nature will find solace there. Binya, a mountain girl, seemed to be the kind of girl who loves nature. She loves wandering in the mountains and valleys. She also enjoys the dark forest and lonely hilltops, and she has no fear there, but she feels nervous and lost in the bazaar crowds. The author showed Binya's love for nature and the environment. By analysing the portrayal of Binya's activities, reveals the author's love for nature. In the flow of the story, Binya finds picnickers while she is returning with her cattle. The picnickers were enjoying their holidays. Binya looked at their clothes, food, and their accents. Binya was quite sturdy, with fair skin, dark eyes, and pinky cheeks. She wore glass bangles and beads around her neck. Here Ruskin showed the classes of the people by their appearances. While crossing the picnickers, she was attracted to the blue umbrella, which belonged to the young lady. They also noticed Binya, and they interacted with her. The young woman was fascinated by Binya's pendant, which created a deep desire in the heart of the young woman. She asked her husband to get it for her. Her husband offered two to five rupees for the pendant, but she refused and expressed her desire for the blue umbrella. The young woman exclaimed as she asked for a beautiful umbrella. The young woman denied this, and this became an argument between the woman and her husband. The small girl is ready to give her lucky pendant, but the woman desires both things. Here, the author shows the adult's covetousness and the child's level of sacrifice. Ruskin portrays their characterization well, as well as two characteristics of children: innocence and a child's love for small things. It shows that children are always happy with what they have. Finally, the woman is ready to exchange the umbrella for the pendant.

The umbrella was compared to a beautiful flower. "The umbrella was like a flower, a great blue flower, that had sprung up on the day brown hillside" (Chapter 1, line 30).

She loved the umbrella so much that even in her house it was opened and placed in a corner. She took the umbrella with her wherever she went to graze the cows, carry milk, or fetch water from the spring. It shows that children have some materialistic fascination. Binya shares her umbrella with others for a little while. She shares her umbrella as a credit to her brother from the mountain to their home, because he gave her sour fruit to eat. The children's mentality is that they give their favourite things to only those they like. Here, Binya thought her umbrella was a precious one, so she shared it with her brother as a credit for his fruits.

The girl sat in the shade of a pine tree one day. The wind picked up the umbrella and made it bounce away from her. After twenty yards, there was a precipice, so she ran faster. The umbrella balanced on the cliff for some time, and then it stuck and hung in the cherry tree. She did not hesitate even for a second and decided to climb the tree. The risk taken by her to take her umbrella shows her love for the umbrella. It also shows her courage and perseverance.

The schoolmaster's wife, the Pujari in the village, and many people there were envious of the beautiful blue umbrella, as no one had ever possessed such a beautiful thing. All were secretly admired for that umbrella, but they never showed up. But the children do not want to pretend to be adults. "Unlike the adults, the children did not have to pretend" (Chapter, line 27).

This line was almost true, as Bond made a beautiful comparison between the children and adults. While crossing the river, she came across a snake, which hisses and prepares to strike. Her blue umbrella was open, and she thrust it between the snake and herself. The snake, using its hard snout, thudded twice. The umbrella thus saved her life as it was a non-living thing. It gives her another life. She told her mother that her love for the umbrella had increased because it had saved her life from the snake.

Ram Bharosa, the important character, and who shares the story equally with Binya, His name means 'Ram the Trustworthy', but here it was the opposite. He runs a tea shop on Tehri Road, which is near Garhwal Hills. By all means, he is the richest man in the village. He lends the things in his shop on credit at the time of calculation. If they can't pay, he charges them extra and snatches some of their valuable things for his personal use or to sell in his shop. Ram Bharosa is greedy for the umbrella; he wants to have it. He offered twelve rupees for that umbrella, but she denied it. It caused a little heartburn for Ram Bharosa. He had an intention of getting that umbrella in anyway. Binya's brother Bijju had to beware of the trick of Ram Bharosa. He already knew about his desire for Binya's umbrella, so he refused his offer. The children's maturity and sacrificing their wishes for their loved ones was nicely expressed by the character Bijju. Bharosa's character Bond showed the man's enviousness of an umbrella. He is rich, but at the same time, he is jealous of that little girl's umbrella. They admire the author for making ordinary things appear extraordinary by showing the richest man envious of them.

Ram Bharosa was employed by Rajaram. He later came to know that it was the desire of Ram towards Binya's umbrella and her rejection to sell it. He decided to make a deal. He asked Bharosa to pay him three rupees for stealing the umbrella and gave more ideas to Ram Bharosa. Thus, the covetousness of Ram Bharosa towards the umbrella and the greediness of Rajaram towards money made them commit a mistake. When Binya was in search of porcupine quills, Rajaram seized the umbrella and ran. Binya was aware of the heavy footsteps and began to run towards them. Bijju, on the other hand, who was collecting a bundle of sticks for the kitchen fire, asked about the happenings. After knowing this, Bijju ran and caught him, and there was a tremendous fight between them. Bijju asked him why he took the umbrella. But Rajaram lied to him that Ram Bharosa had asked him to fetch this umbrella, otherwise he would lose his job. He takes Ram Bharosa's name and his well-known obsession with the umbrella; everybody believes the lie. The whole village stops visiting his shop, and he falls into great misery. He had suffered the tortures of greed, hatred from the side of the village people, and the despair of loneliness. While passing the shop of Bharosa and his condition, Binya thinks that she is only responsible for this misery. Her reasoning towards herself stood out as the most beautiful part. She thinks that he loved the umbrella too much, which made her forget other people's happiness and she failed to give importance to the people around her because of her unconditional love for the umbrella. She thinks that she was the only one to notice Ram Bharosa's shop in such a condition. There was no doubt that it was totally Ram's greediness, but she felt too bad for her doings. She didn't want to feel this, but it showed her character of goodness and kindness. The lines, "Had she loved the umbrella too much? Had it mattered more to her than people mattered?" is lingering in her thoughts.

Through her compassionate heart, she discovers there is more to life than material possessions. Finally, she decided to sacrifice her most lovable umbrella and kept it in the shop at Ram Bharosa. He went back to her and asked her why she left. She said that she doesn't need that umbrella anymore and asked to keep it with her.

Ruskin Bond concludes, "But an umbrella isn't everything." (Chapter 6, line 47). Ram Bharosa sacrifices her umbrella for the happiness of Ram Binya. And this, in turn, makes him a more pleasant and friendly person. It is an example of how the simple act of kindness can indeed transform lives.

People started visiting Ram Bharosa's shop after Binya's gift of the beautiful blue umbrella. It was opened outside, and whoever wants it can borrow and use it. This humble act of kindness leads Ram Bharosa to gift Binya a bear-claw pendant on a silver chain, considered even luckier than her leopard-claw pendant.

The whole set of events arouses every emotion in this story, such as love, possession, fulfilment, temptation, greed, pride, fear, regret, loneliness, happiness, viciousness, care, and selfless motives. This story provokes the innermost child in an adult reader.

It is to understand how human values stand above materialistic substances. Learning the art of accurately appraising is one of the great arts of learning. Everything has its own value in terms of what one thinks, learns, and gives out in any way that touches the consciousness own value. These values are apt to change with the mood, with time, or because of circumstances. It cannot be safely tied to any material value. The values of all material possessions change continually, sometimes overnight. Nothing of this nature has any permanent set value. The real values are those that stay and give happiness and enrichment. They are human values. None of those material possessions do anything to make life any better. There are a lot of people who have everything. They're the most miserable people in the world. So, it won't do anything unless they get happy and can have peace within themselves.

Reference

A Walk with Ruskin Bond. Navneet speaks. N.p., 27 Jan. 2017. Web. 15 Dec. 2018.

Abhi2400. "The Blue Umbrella Reviews and Ratings." Mouthshut.com. N.p., 11 Sept. 2008. Web. 14

Bond, Ruskin. *My Writings Reflect My Lonely Childhood*. News18. News18, 09 Apr. 2014. Web. 02Dec. 2018.

Bond, Ruskin. *The Ruskin Bond Children's Omnibus*: Rupa. Co., 1995.

https://www.hindustantimes.com/. Hindustan Times, 10 Aug. 2007. Web.02 Dec. 2018.

Tales of Innocence and Experience a Thematic Study of Ruskin Bonds Selected Works.09-chapter 5.

Walk the Talk with Ruskin Bond. NDTV.com. NDTV, 24 Nov. 2012. Web. 15 Dec, 2018.

List Of Contributors

Throughout the creation of this book, "Literary Sprouts" relied heavily on the contributions of students and scholars. Their contributions are really invaluable, and I would like to take a moment to thank them and recognise them for all of their hard work.

Abina Blessy. D - Infant Jesus College of Arts and Science for Women.

Ajitha Robin. I - Infant Jesus College of Arts and Science for Women.

S. Ambika - Edayathangudy G. S. Pillay Arts & Science College (Autonomous).

Amos Dishonraj. A - Edayathangudy G. S. Pillay Arts & Science College (Autonomous).

I. Ashika - Edayathangudy G. S. Pillay Arts & Science College (Autonomous).

M.S. Atchaya - Edayathangudy G. S. Pillay Arts & Science College (Autonomous).

S. Beghin Bose - S.T. Hindu College (Affiliated to M.S. University).

T. Deepalakshmi - Edayathangudy G. S. Pillay Arts & Science College (Autonomous).

G. Dharani - Swami Dayananda College of Arts & Science, Manjakkudi.

A. Durgadevi - Edayathangudy G. S. Pillay Arts & Science College (Autonomous).

R. Indhu - St. Xavier College of Education.

R. Karthikayini - Edayathangudy G. S. Pillay Arts & Science College (Autonomous).

K. Kiruthika - Swami Dayananda College of Arts and Science.

K. Lawanya - Swami Dayananda College of Arts and Science.

R. Madubala - Edayathangudy G. S. Pillay Arts & Science College (Autonomous).

Misma. S - Infant Jesus College of Arts and Science for Women.

M. Monisha - Edayathangudy G. S. Pillay Arts & Science College (Autonomous).

Ragavi. G - Edayathangudy G. S. Pillay Arts & Science College (Autonomous).

M.Sailaxmi - Edayathangudy G. S. Pillay Arts & Science College (Autonomous).

M. Shanmathi - Rabiammal Ahamed Maideen College for Women.

Shimna. S - Infant Jesus College of Arts and Science for Women.

K. Siva Dharshni - Edayathangudy G. S. Pillay Arts & Science College (Autonomous).

M. Suganya - Edayathangudy G. S. Pillay Arts & Science College (Autonomous).

V. Swerna Malika - Edayathangudy G. S. Pillay Arts & Science College (Autonomous).

L.B. Thamil Yazhini - Bon Secours College for Women.

Thasneem. S - Edayathangudy G. S. Pillay Arts & Science College (Autonomous).

K.A.Yazhini - Edayathangudy G. S. Pillay Arts & Science College (Autonomous).

M. Yuvarani & E. Ganga - Government College for Women (Autonomous).

9 798887 838311

Printed by Libri Plureos GmbH in Hamburg,
Germany